The Complete Guide to

SELLING
yourself

IN TODAY'S COMPETITIVE MARKETPLACE

Thomas A. Freese

Published by:

QBS Publishing, Inc.
P.O. Box 922933
Atlanta, Georgia 30010-2933
tfreese@QBSresearch.com

From the Bestselling Author of:
Secrets of Question Based Selling
It Only Takes 1% to Have a Competitive Edge in Sales
The New Era of Salesmanship
The Question Based Parent

QBS™, Question Based Selling™, PAS Positioning™, Diagnostic Questions™, Conversational Layering™, and Conversational Dynamics™ are all trademarks of QBS Research, Inc.

1st printing 2009
Printed in Canada
Library of Congress Control Number: 2009904598
ISBN: 978-1-891892-66-0

Cover design by Warren Caldwell and Craig Moonshower
Book design by Craig Moonshower

*This book is dedicated to
"Big Red," the person (on the cover)
who is ready to take control
of their own success.*

Acknowledgements

For me, the best thing to come out of the recent economic turmoil is a renewed sense of purpose, helping potential and existing clients reexamine how they conduct business, and in many cases, reinventing their sales approach. In fact, I have been fortunate on this project to be surrounded by a world class team of professionals, and all around good folks, as this (my fifth) book was definitely a collaborative effort.

Let me start by thanking my friend and marketing guru, Scott Whitney. In addition to building the best websites on the planet, Scott's expertise and experience as a podcaster and master of live streaming video has enabled us to create QBS "Live" Mondays—a free, biweekly Internet broadcast that provides live interactive QBS coaching in addition to keeping listeners updated on new QBS techniques.

The unsung hero on this project is my Executive Assistant, Robin Decker. In addition to being a rock of sanity when things get crazy, her quiet confidence continues to inspire me on a daily basis, and her dedication to helping clients in every way possible is incomparable. I also wish to thank Alan Rohrer and Jim Russell for their commitment to delivering QBS Methodology Training at the highest level.

Regarding design, layout, and the finished product that you are holding in your hands, many accolades go to my publishing tandem of Craig Moonshower and Warren Caldwell, whose vision and professionalism have once again proven that two heads are better than one. I would also like to thank my editor-in-chief, Laura Freese, along with Emily Gilreath (my proof reader-in-chief), whose combined editing contributions have convinced me that four heads are better than two. Lastly, on the publishing front, I want to give an appreciative shout-out to my literary agent-in-chief, Al Zuckerman, who has always believed in me.

A special note of gratitude to goes to a handful of special people (in no particular order), including Mark Reed, Gregg Quisito, Jerry Saunders, Jarrett McConnico, Monte Mickle, Evan Steiner, Vaughn Rachal, Mathew Gore, Steve Johnson, Mark Selleck, Barry Gillman, Dan Hess, Paul Owens, Steele Faust, Jake Sanchez, Jim Hardee, Mitch Little, Mike Henderson, Danny Jones, Tom Mathews, Mike Fogerty, Terry Edge, Larry Freese, Richard Sites, Bart Burton, Bill Burton, and Charlie King. I simply cannot put into words the positive impact these people have had on my work and on the resulting success I have experienced over the years.

Last but not least, I want to thank my wife Laura for her unconditional support throughout my entire QBS journey, and to my girls, Sarah and Mary Claire. Truth be known, my two daughters are without a doubt the best salespeople in the Freese household.

Table of Contents

Preface

You are always selling yourself.

In 1992, when I first sat down with Jeff Hudson, Senior Vice President of Worldwide Sales, to interview for a territory sales position with NetFrame Systems, he asked me, *"Tom, do you think you would be successful selling NetFrame superserver technology?"*

It would have been tempting to look him square in the eye, and confidently answer, "Yes, absolutely!" You had to assume other candidates who were competing for the position probably responded that way, followed by a lengthy diatribe about their best personal attributes and their many accomplishments.

Instead, I answered his question in a different way. I said, *"Well, I'm not sure how to assess my potential at NetFrame since I've never sold superservers before. But, given that you have a great deal of experience in the business, how about I share my sales philosophy, and my plan of attack, and then maybe you could tell me if you think I would be successful?"* Jeff smiled knowingly. I did too.

I proceeded to describe my philosophy on selling, including many of the techniques I explain in this book. Rather than just bragging about how great I was and making him wonder how I would actually approach the opportunity, I figured that if I gave Jeff a glimpse into what my strategy was for being successful in the job, then he could assess for himself how 'great' I was.

Less than an hour after I returned home the next morning on the red-eye flight from San Francisco, a FedEx truck pulled up to my house and delivered a generous job offer to my front door. Apparently, Jeff must have thought I would be successful selling superservers. Turns out, I was.

The rest is history.

Introduction

Selling Yourself In Today's Competitive Marketplace is not just the title of this book. Rather, it's the challenge we all now face given that the game has changed—starting with the fact that it's no longer a *game*. Your long-term career aspirations, along with your day to day livelihood, will depend on your own personal effectiveness, now more than ever. Even if you're not a career salesperson, whether you manage a small business, support the organization in a customer service role, or you are an executive in a Fortune 500 company, you are definitely *selling yourself* every day.

Honestly, it's easy to sell when business conditions are favorable. For the better part of two generations, we have enjoyed an unprecedented run of good times. The economy has boomed, rampant spending has become an accepted part of our culture, and ravenous growth has distorted the corporate mindset to the point where just a few quarters ago, companies couldn't hire new employees fast enough. More was definitely better. Then, reality set in and the bubble burst.

Though life is still pretty good for most people, justifying your value to your company and to your customers is not going to be as easy as before. The fact that you are reading this book tells me you are committed to excellence in your chosen profession. I must assume, however, that some of your toughest competitors are similarly devoted to their success. Even if you are indeed a capable individual, it's unlikely that you are the only talented person in your industry. Companies offering similar solutions will be competing against you to gain the customer's trust and ultimately to earn their business. Someone is eventually going to win these battles, and, as you might expect with any competitive situation, your ability to succeed has a lot to do with *you*.

Most of the salespeople I train are veterans. Once in a while we encounter a group of 'newbies' fresh out of college, but for the most part, the audiences we see on a weekly basis are filled with experienced professionals who are looking for something constructive and practical that will give them a competitive advantage.

Selling Yourself is the next logical step in a journey that began twelve years ago when I introduced the QBS Methodology and published my first book, *Secrets of Question Based Selling*. Since that time, QBS has been adopted by thousands of salespeople, managers, and sales support professionals all over the world. QBS Research, Inc. has also become the recognized thought-leader for 'new era' sales effectiveness training and courseware.

Ironically, the notion of *selling yourself* has been an elusive concept within traditional sales models for many years. People used to think personality and charm were the most essential ingredients to being successful in sales. It was also believed that you were either born to be a salesperson, or you weren't. We now know nothing could be further from the truth. Customers these days are not impressed when a smooth-talker shows up peddling a slate of goods or services, and prospective buyers are increasingly reluctant to share information with someone they don't yet know or trust, anyway.

For too long, companies have been content to arm their sales teams with some basic product training before sending them out into their territories to talk about features and benefits. However, product differentiation is only a good strategy if your product or service is capable of selling itself. For example, in the future, when someone comes out with an affordable flying car, that type of product could potentially sell itself! Likewise, whoever stumbles upon a cure for breast cancer won't need to be a marketing genius to generate tons of revenue from eager clients.

Given the current business climate, however, sellers can no longer count on their products alone to be the differentiator. The more likely scenario is that you will encounter competitors who offer comparable solutions, which customers perceive as functionally equivalent. For example, what do you suppose the real difference is between Allstate, State Farm, and Nationwide Insurance? I guess it comes down to whether you want to be "in good hands," "have a good neighbor," or like the idea of having Nationwide "on your side." From a pure product perspective, there's not much difference between the three. The same can be said of the entire financial services industry, as you can purchase the same exact shares of General Electric or Coca-Cola stock from any number of brokerage houses, often located within blocks of each other. Realtors face a similar challenge, as they are all essentially competing to market and sell the same inventory of homes at the same listed price. Even the drug companies face stiffer competition as a continuous pipeline of new formulary alternatives comes on the market.

When rival companies battle to out-describe each other, comparable solutions tend to get commoditized and often end up sounding very much the same to end-customers. When this occurs, you can no longer count on the product itself for differentiation, as everyone claims to offer the best solutions.

Don't get me wrong, the image of your company and the quality of your product offering is definitely important. But, in most industries, the person representing a product or service is likely to have a greater influence on the customer's perception than the product itself.

For example, if you open a brokerage account with a firm like Morgan Stanley, you will probably never cross paths with Mr. Morgan or Mr. Stanley. Instead, your confidence in the company would almost exclusively be the result of a relationship you develop with one of their sixteen thousand financial advisors. To you, the financial advisor *is* the company. This same phenomenon applies in almost every business, whether you are selling real estate, or you are a manufacturer's rep, pharmaceutical salesperson, technology integrator, accountant, engineer, attorney, financial planner, builder, consultant, franchisee, or a sales trainer. The effectiveness of the salesperson will definitely impact the customer's perception of the products and services being offered.

> "The person representing a product or service is likely to have a greater influence on the customer's perception than the product itself."

Once companies began to take this idea of individual sales performance seriously, the initial spotlight in corporate training focused on reengineering the sales process. Hence, the 1990's became a 'gold rush' of sorts for consultants and sales process vendors, as client corporations deployed programs like Strategic Selling, SPIN Selling, and Solution Selling at a feverish pace. While redefining the steps of the sales process can absolutely help improve forecast consistency and create a common language, formalizing your internal sales process no longer gives sales teams a competitive advantage. By now, most of your competitors have a process in place as well, and it's safe to assume that the steps of their sales process are virtually identical to yours. So, what makes *you* stand out from the competition?

To me, it doesn't make sense to teach sellers to sound just like their competitors. That was always my frustration as a salesperson. Sounding the same as everyone else is the quickest way to commoditize your value. It's also a sure way to lengthen the sales cycle, erode your company's profit margins, and lower your probability of being selected. Also, since buyers have become more sophisticated, most of the old-school sales tricks and gimmicks that were once used to try and persuade customers are pretty much destined to fail.

Selling Yourself in Today's Competitive Marketplace is about boosting your sales effectiveness, plain and simple. If you look around any sales organization, you will quickly discover that some salespeople are more effective than others, even when they are selling the same products to essentially the same target audience. What separates these top performing salespeople from their struggling counterparts? Let me give you the answer to this question in two words—customer perception.

Your success in business and in life will ultimately hinge on the impressions other people form about *you*. If you sell for a living, then you already understand that customers are always forming impressions, and their perception of *you* will largely determine whether or not they choose to purchase your product or service. Thus, closely contested sales opportunities usually come down to a host of intangibles, which include a variety of attributes like the salesperson's credibility, expertise, knowledge, vision, helpfulness, respect, honesty, customer-focus, and their consistency in following through on verbal commitments. The extent to which you possess these character traits is not even the issue. The challenge is being able to effectively convey these intangible qualities to enhance the value you bring to customers, partners, colleagues, and your management chain.

To me, the notion that our success is largely determined by our own effectiveness is terrific news. This gives you the power to control your own destiny, either to step up and enhance your ability to convey value, or to continue with the status quo.

My goal for this book was to create a repeatable formula for selling yourself, which extends beyond the notion that readers would simply take a few pearls of wisdom away from the text. Ultimately, you need a system that supports the effective implementation of the softer skills—skills like piquing the customer's interest, establishing your own credibility, building relationships, differentiating your solutions, justifying cost, and securing commitments. In fact, I would argue that skills development has become the new field on which the *game* of selling is now being played. At the end of the day, customers are going to turn to someone for advice and it's reasonable to assume it's either going to be you or a competitor. Hence, there is some responsibility on your part to decide how you want to be perceived, and then to be proactive enough to implement a repeatable strategy that will enable you to achieve the desired result.

That said, you may want to fasten your seat belt and get ready for perhaps the most intensive intellectual ride of your sales career. Just as *Secrets of Question Based Selling* was an intentional departure from traditional sales methods, we will spend a fair amount of time in this book undoing many of the prevailing sales theories that have been taught to salespeople over the years. My litmus test regarding legitimate sales strategies is relatively simple. If something is not likely to work when a salesperson approaches me or you, then it's safe to presume it probably won't work on other discerning customers, either.

On a personal note, I am grateful to have had the opportunity to share my ideas on selling with so many salespeople, managers, executives, and non-salespeople. I am also humbled by the eagerness these people have shown over the years to implement the Question Based Selling methodology and to refer QBS and our training programs to others. Thank you for placing such confidence in me. To that end, my mantra for this book is relatively simple. When selling yourself, do only those things that make sense. Make sure you always have a purpose. And, allow logic and reasonability to always be your guide.

Now, grab your favorite highlighter and prepare for an odyssey that will change the way you deal with customers moving forward. With absolute confidence I can tell you that *Selling Yourself in Today's Competitive Marketplace* will absolutely change the way customers perceive and deal with *you*.

Chapter 1

The Perfect Storm

More than at any other time since the industrial revolution, companies and individuals in all industries are looking for ways to retain customers, boost top-line revenue, and maintain profit margins. To survive and ultimately flourish in this new economy, we must reexamine the way we deal with customers; and some of the adjustments that need to be made are long overdue.

The sales function is the lifeblood of every organization, and true sales effectiveness is no longer optional. As a result, a Darwinian-style recalibration is underway, and the sales professional will play a more crucial role in their own success than ever before.

Everything seems eerily different now, as we slowly come to grips with the reality that the field on which we work and play has changed dramatically. Even those of us who were minding our own business when the downturn began breathed a collective gasp as the era of unabated growth and prosperity that our economy has enjoyed over the last thirty years seemed to collapse overnight. Not since the nineteen thirties have we experienced a scenario that could so widely impact the financial, political, and social fabric of our country, where the changing economic landscape will inevitably impact everyone at some point, if it hasn't affected you already.

We have essentially been 'snow-globed.' We've been turned upside down and shaken to the point where the tranquil scenes of our daily existence have been shrouded by a flurry of uncertainty that has suddenly clouded our view, and little pieces of reality now seem to be raining down in all directions.

Who would have thought that our banking system would need a trillion-dollar bailout, or that Wall Street brokerage houses could go out of business over a weekend? Consumer debt levels are at an all-time high, many home mortgages are upside down, and it will take some time for new construction to ramp back up to previous levels. Meanwhile, 'the big three' automobile manufacturers in the United States are no where near as "big" as they once were, unemployment has attained century-long high water marks, and the job market for skilled workers and professionals has tightened significantly. These factors have all come together at the same time to create a *perfect storm* of economic conditions that has sent our previous capitalistic mindset into a veritable tailspin.

When sales are up and the economy is flourishing, people tend to be fat and happy. After such a long run of prosperity, however, we unfortunately forgot some of the basic fundamentals, like diversifying our investment portfolios or saving for a rainy day. For whatever reason, our sense of reasonability floated off into the distance like dandelion seeds on a spring day. When times were good, if you wanted something you simply bought it. If you didn't have enough money, you bought it anyway, holding onto the belief that the money train would surely never end. Well, those days have definitely ended.

I see it in the eyes of audience participants during some of the QBS training programs I've recently delivered. People are naturally worried. Some of them should be. I'm not trying to be insensitive, just realistic. The jig is up; the news is out, and no matter which metaphoric reference you like best, I suspect that this genie isn't going back in the bottle anytime soon.

You will soon discover that I'm not one of those doomsdayers who runs around predicting economic Armageddon, nor do I believe we are headed for another Great Depression. We will survive this current downturn, in addition to the various humps and bumps that will likely occur as part of any economic recovery. That said, I would argue that we have entered a historic period that could one day come to be known as 'The Great Adjustment.' From my perspective, a complete recalibration by businesses and individuals is now underway, and I suspect that some of the lessons learned over the next few years will be administered by the school of hard knocks.

The good news is, the situation initially deteriorated so rapidly that most people recognized the seriousness of the downturn and acknowledged the impending need for action. Just pick up any newspaper or tune into the pundits on cable television, and it's clear that no one believes this adjustment is just a passing fancy. Whether you look at recent consumer confidence surveys, debt to equity ratios, budget cuts, layoffs, or the degree of government intervention, our once abounding economic optimism has quite noticeably been transformed into a holistic sense of uncertainty regarding the future.

Looking back on thirty years of unbridled opulence, there is probably a whole generation (or two) that has never experienced what my grandfather, who lived through the depression era, used to call "tough times." For years we've conditioned ourselves to do whatever we pleased, oftentimes by mortgaging our future in exchange for shorter term gains. Truthfully, we have become a soft culture—a society of doing whatever we want to do as opposed to doing what truly needs to be done.

My purpose here is not to criticize your standard of living or condemn anyone's lifestyle choices up to this point. I am merely pointing out a cultural phenomenon—when economic conditions are too good for too long, life gets easy and complacency tends to set in.

From a business perspective, there was little need to worry about personal effectiveness or retooling your skills because everything seemed to be humming along just fine. While it may be a little ironic to say, this sudden disruption to our previous feelings of exuberance and contentment may just be the silver lining that will give us the opportunity to leapfrog out of this current economic turbulence.

Am I the only one who thinks there have been a few times in recent history where we could've used a good kick in the pants? If the world ends tomorrow, then it won't really matter if you have a strategic plan in place, or not. If, however, the world does not come to an end in the next day or two (the more likely scenario), I believe you will see a reemergence of the familiar Darwinian paradigm, 'Survival of the Fittest,' which will separate those people who have superior capability, skills, and top performance, from the rest of the pretenders in the marketplace. Thus, there has never been a better time to pay attention with regard to how you conduct yourself, because the coming months and the next few years will likely determine where you end up when the dust settles and the current turbulence subsides.

The Appetite for Change has Never Been Greater

When "the pie" is relatively large and there's more than enough business for everyone in the marketplace, sales meetings transform into celebratory festivals where everyone congratulates themselves on a job well done. Then, one day, the size of the pie unexpectedly shrinks and suddenly there's no longer enough business to go around. The resulting mood at these meetings abruptly shifts from congratulations and self-indulgence to a more serious tone, with a sense of urgency to find ways to adjust to rapidly changing market conditions.

Like a real-life game of musical chairs, it has become clear to me that *not* everyone will get a seat when the music stops. And, even those who are able to withstand and survive the tumultuous nature of today's competitive marketplace will undoubtedly notice that the slices of pie coming their way have become appreciably smaller.

Guess what happens when salespeople and companies begin to transact smaller and smaller pieces of business, or in some cases, they are no longer getting any portions of the pie at all? When times are tough, companies as well as individual salespeople become perceptibly hungrier. One could say our survival instincts kick in, which ratchets up competitive pressure in the marketplace, as salespeople ramp up their efforts to fight for every morsel of opportunity in their respective industries. Struggling vendor representatives who are not able to differentiate themselves or their products will inevitably resort to significantly discounting their prices, thus eroding profit margins even further. Sound familiar?

On the other hand, this increased pressure in the marketplace comes with an ironic upside, one that has sparked a renewed sense of desire within companies, and, I dare say, throughout the entire sales profession. It turns out that the same people who are hungry for business are also eager for a new perspective and creative ideas about what they can and should do differently. Never before have individual salespeople been so willing to put their egos aside and adjust their approach to make themselves invaluable to their company and customers. I remember a time not so long ago when sellers would actually come to my class without a pad or pencil, fold their arms, roll their eyes, and hope the clock would soon roll ahead to the end of day so they could head to the gym. Those days are gone, as sellers are much more willing to invest in themselves and reexamine their current sales approach. Have you heard the saying: *There are no atheists on a turbulent fight, or in the waiting area at a children's hospital?* Most salespeople are smart enough to realize that some adjustments are necessary with regard to how we deal with clients, as it now appears that our best opportunity to get out of the current predicament is going to be to somehow sell our way out.

> "Never before have individual salespeople been so willing to put their egos aside and adjust their approach to make themselves invaluable to their company and customers."

Companies have experienced a bit of a come-uppance as well, where much of the typical squabbling and internal politics that have traditionally plagued organizations has been replaced by an 'all hands on deck' mentality. Essentially, the same perfect storm that recently stirred up so much dust in the marketplace has also fostered a 'perfect opportunity' to recalibrate the traditional selling mindset.

Recalibrating your sales force doesn't have to be as daunting as it sounds. However, some training departments will need to shift their focus away from continually redefining the sales process or launching anything that can be characterized as a refresher course. Teaching salespeople to sound just like your competition is pointless, and anything that merits the title of a 'refresher' course is more likely to send people backward in their thinking rather than forward.

If you agree that one of the keys to adjusting to this new environment involves a willingness to adapt to a changing competitive landscape, then I would argue that your success moving forward is not only contingent on the execution of a sound business strategy, but also on the implementation of excellent sales technique. To accomplish this, some guidance and direction will surely be necessary, as the path to success in the new economy is going to be very different than what we were accustomed to when everyone was fat and happy.

It's strange to me that sales drives the success of every company, yet the skills required to be successful in a sales role continue to be the least taught professional discipline in the world. Many companies still rely on individual salespeople to educate themselves. The more experienced sellers on your team may have attended a smattering of sales courses over the years, but learning how to sell during prosperous economic times is still very different than understanding how to be effective in sales when times are tough.

Given enough time and tribulation, I suppose an industrious salesperson could figure out how to make some of the necessary adjustments on their own. Frankly, there's nothing magical or secretive about the strategies and techniques you will learn in this book. Most companies and sales managers don't have the luxury of time, however, which limits the plausibility of a sales development strategy that's based on the hope that people will "eventually" learn from trial and error. While salespeople can absolutely learn from each other, the real opportunity is for companies to do something that will raise the tide for the entire sales organization, and it needs to happen soon.

Emphasis on Sales Effectiveness

Who (exactly) should be faulted for the recent slump in sales? Pointing fingers to assign blame has become a national pastime in some parts of the world. However, in sales, after you get done blaming the economy, the corporate marketing department, the competition, and sometimes even blaming the customer, if you look around any sales organization, you will notice that some salespeople are more effective than others, selling the exact same products and services to the same types of customers.

What is it that makes top performers more effective than their colleagues? What are they doing to separate themselves from the competition, and overcome the adversities and grievances that other salespeople see as obstacles?

As I have become older, and I hope wiser, I have definitely become more direct in my dealings with people. I tend to be very straight-forward when communicating with customers, and I definitely tell it like it is when teaching salespeople how to be more effective. I'm not sure why it's not more common to communicate in this manner, but I know from experience that most QBS students appreciate straight talk.

In that vein, this book was intentionally and unmistakably written to increase the sales effectiveness of the person staring back at you when you look in the mirror. It is possible that the techniques and strategies outlined in this book will also help your colleagues, your business partners, or maybe even your boss. Let's call that a bonus if it happens. But, rather than looking elsewhere for answers, I am going to suggest that it's now time for individuals to take matters into their own hands with regard to selling yourself.

Honestly, it's easy to sell lots of stuff when the economy is booming and everyone has money, or if you sell a product or service that enjoys significant functional advantages over the competition. But, what happens when the playing field unexpectedly gets leveled, and you realize that most salespeople are used to selling in an up market?

Unfortunately, the whole topic of sales effectiveness has been pushed to the back burner for too long, and lots of people have unexpectedly been caught with their pants down. Who is responsible for the current state of the economy? Perhaps the better question is, who is going to be responsible for your success moving forward? Focusing on how we got to this point isn't going to suddenly change your skill set or move pending opportunities forward in your sales pipeline toward closure.

The realization that the ball is now in your court does have a significant upside, however. Simply put, necessity has always been the mother of invention. If it's true that some salespeople in your industry are more effective than others, than I encourage you to bring sales effectiveness back to the forefront, in order to put yourself in a stronger position to be perceived as a more valuable resource by your company and your customers. You do this by learning how to win the sale when the customer's decision comes down to a virtual tie between vendors.

Learn to Win the Ties

Most of the sales training that has been delivered over the past couple of decades has focused on how to exploit your product's unique value proposition. Consequently, salespeople have become very dependent on bullet points, product brochures, benchmark tests, and live demonstrations to show how much better their solutions are than competitive offerings. But, what if the product or service you sell doesn't actually have a dramatic functional advantage, or a "unique" value proposition?

One of the recent casualties of this rapidly changing marketplace is commoditization. Now that sellers are having to fight harder and harder to win each sale, the natural competitive instincts that kick in cause salespeople to be more and more aggressive in touting the value of their solutions. Call it desperation, but companies in lean times tend to make more emphatic claims with regard to their products in the hopes of influencing customer purchasing decisions. Meanwhile, the targets of this aggression (decision makers) end up receiving a steady stream of "desperate" sales calls from hungry vendors, all wanting to offer a special 'once in a lifetime' deal that will transform the customer's business or somehow change their life forever.

Of course, the pure volume and extremity of these offers tends to undermine the credibility and validity of the claims being made. Think about it this way: Are you impressed when you see a weight-loss commercial on television claiming that you can lose thirty pounds in one week, without exercise or cutting back on what you eat? As a cautious consumer yourself, I bet you assume that most of these outlandish claims from vendors are considerably overstated, which is exactly my point.

Additionally, many of the discretionary "nice-to-have" features of a product or service have now taken a back seat to a significantly smaller list of "absolute must-haves." As a result, much of the value vendors are accustomed to highlighting is being commoditized simply because budget conscious decision makers are realizing they don't necessarily need (or can no longer afford) all the bells and whistles. Customers battling difficult market conditions have also hunkered down and it's no longer important or fashionable for decision makers to insist on the fastest or most fabulous product options available.

For example, people who used to buy the Mercedes Benz of a certain offering are realizing that they can be just as happy with the Toyota equivalent, especially if it accomplishes the same objective. Similarly, people who used to shop at Neiman Marcus are now finding much of what they need at Macy's or even Target. Thus, if you have become dependent on functional advantages to sell your product, and you are now selling in an environment where purchase decisions no longer revolve around the need for superior bells and whistles, your competitive advantage may have been dramatically reduced. When this occurs, customers often default to a lesser solution that is still workable, but significantly lower in price. Where does that leave your current value proposition and your potential solutions?

Another casualty of this *New Era of Salesmanship* (the title of my third book) is the erosion of existing client relationships, and the deteriorating impact personal friendships are now having on purchase decisions. It used to be true that if someone liked you, they purchased your product or service. We do want customers to like us and it is perfectly acceptable to forge personal relationships with your favorite clients. I continue to stay in touch with several people where our friendship originated within client accounts many years ago. But once again, as the backdrop of our new market reality changes, the ability to count on winning business simply because you are friends with someone in the account is rapidly dwindling.

Rampant reorganization along with recent merger and acquisition activity, natural attrition, and layoffs have reshuffled the cards in many existing customer accounts, to the point where your next call into a previously friendly contact could very well turn into a 'cold call' to someone else who holds no loyalties toward you whatsoever. At the same time, vendors who are also trying to adapt to market conditions have similarly reshuffled their organizations, putting people into new positions and changing their go-to-market strategies. Either of these scenarios now presents a serious challenge for salespeople and companies who used to make a comfortable living just by farming pet accounts during the boom years.

Case in point, fifty years ago in North America, it would actually have been considered inappropriate to open a sales conversation with a relevant business purpose. That's because being successful in sales was once thought to revolve almost exclusively around the idea of fostering personal relationships. Hence, the quintessential salesperson has always been looked upon as a congenial glad-hander with a fake smile and a forced laugh after every punctuation mark.

These days, the opposite approach to dealing with

customers is more likely to prevail. Now, the most valuable salesperson is the one who is perceived by customers as being purposeful, relevant, valuable, and knowledgeable. Integrity and credibility go hand-in-hand with this new brand of salesperson and their goals extend way beyond just making a sale, as they focus specifically on addressing the customer's needs and making the best use of the decision maker's time.

From my perspective, this shift from being a glad-hander to being perceived by customers as a valuable resource is a welcome change in terms of selling yourself. In fact, I can tell you right now that this is not a book about how to be friendly or effusive. At this point, let's assume that most of your customers have enough friends already. My focus and life's work is about teaching salespeople and sales organizations how to position themselves in a manner that makes then more valuable in the eyes of potential decision makers, as opposed to sounding like every other sales caller. Especially now, if you are not seen as a valuable resource in the eyes of your target audience, decision makers probably won't want to deal with you at all.

If your product or service is something customers actually do need, then you should still be able to generate sales even under difficult economic conditions. The challenge comes when the playing field gets leveled and your value proposition suddenly gets commoditized by competitive market forces. To be successful in this environment, sellers must stop relying on product features or depending on functional advantages. Instead, you must learn how to win the business even when the decision comes down to a virtual tie between yourself and your closest competitor, which includes the decision to do nothing and maintain the status quo.

Most People Don't Buy the Cheapest

The primary reason to employ salespeople is to make sure that your value proposition does not get commoditized in a competitive market, and to ensure important aspects of your solution get noticed by potential buyers. The good news is, most customers aren't looking for the cheapest possible alternative. Cost is definitely an important decision factor these days. But, if you think about it, most people don't drive the cheapest car, eat the cheapest food, nor do they wear the cheapest clothes. Instead, customers today are interested in choosing whichever option provides the greatest value.

> "Whether or not customers choose to deal with you has a lot to do with how you choose to deal with them."

Whether or not customers end up perceiving that your product, service, or company offers the most value has a great deal to do with their perception of *you* as a valuable resource. Put it this way, if you are indeed valuable to the customer, and can consistently be perceived as such, you will have plenty of friends in your client accounts.

Even so, chances are good that you are not the only person in your industry that adds value. That's fine. Even if an equivalent product can be purchased from a competitor, like in real estate sales, where the same property can be purchased from any number of licensed real estate agents at the same price, you will find that customers usually don't deal with just anyone. Instead, they chose to work with the person or company who provides the greatest value. The same logic applies in most competitive markets, whether you sell financial services, pharmaceuticals, technology, or sales training courseware.

Customers are ultimately going to partner with someone, and whether or not they choose to deal with you has a lot to do with how you choose to deal with them. Therefore, I can tell you right now that the difference between winning and losing the customer's business is likely to come down to their perception of *you*.

My New Favorite Sales Movie

Believe it or not, I have a new favorite sales movie. Ironically, it's not one of those Hollywood action thrillers. Rather, it's a family classic that has endured the test of time to become one of the most popular and most watched motion pictures in history. Have you seen *The Wizard of Oz*? I've lost count of how many times I've watched this flick over the years. Just recently, I decided it was my new favorite sales movie of all time.

The movie has everything—drama, suspense, music, humor, and dancing, along with a smattering of early special effects that together, suspend the audience's reality for almost two full hours. The movie portrays an epic battle between good and evil, as Dorothy (the main character) personally experiences what it means to find knowledge, heart, and c-c-courage, right in her own backyard. It's a film that evokes both tears and joy, no matter whether you are a child seeing it for the first time, or you make a perennial visit to Munchkin-land.

Want to know why *The Wizard of Oz* has become my new favorite sales movie of all time? Trust me; it hasn't always been my favorite. I used to think it was a story was about a girl who was just having a bad day after being conked on the head during a terrible storm. Then, just recently, I started to notice an interesting parallel between the storyline in *The Wizard of Oz* and a typical sales situation.

Maybe you remember the single most important scene in the film, where the entire plot reveals itself to the characters in the story, and to the movie audience. It happens when Dorothy's dog Toto pulls back the curtain and we suddenly discover that the great and powerful Wizard of Oz is just a regular person. "Pay no attention to that man behind the curtain," the deafening voice booms over the loudspeaker. Once the Great Oz is revealed to everyone for who he truly is, the story takes an interesting twist and the movie resolves itself shortly thereafter. I won't spoil the ending for you if you haven't seen it.

This memorable movie scene forever captures the number one concern buyers everywhere have when dealing with salespeople and vendors—they want to know what's really going on *behind the curtain.*

As buyers ourselves, we understand sellers are eager to point out all the wonderful benefits offered by their products and services. However, we also know all too well that there is no such thing as a perfect solution. In fact, we have learned through experience that products usually have advantages and disadvantages, pros and cons, strengths and weaknesses. Have you ever made a purchase you thought was great, but ended up being a bad decision once you got it home and the rest of the story was revealed?

As it turns out, prospective customers aren't just looking for a sterile accounting of features and benefits when talking with vendor representatives. What they really want is to gain a comfort level that comes from certain intangibles that don't necessarily show up on the pages of a vendor's printed product brochure or appear as bullet points on a corporate slide presentation. Discerning customers are looking for things like knowl-edge, integrity, value, leadership, vision, experience, thought leadership, innovation, creativity, helpfulness, and someone who simply cares about the customer's needs. Whether they verbalize it or not, these traits are extremely important to most decision makers. When the time for a decision arrives, customers want to know they are dealing with someone who cares about their success *after* the sale, and they want to feel comfortable that you have the depth and perspective to offer sound advice that will help them make good decisions.

The challenge for sellers is, how exactly is one supposed to display these highly intangible character traits? Personal qualities like knowledge, integrity, value, leadership, vision, experience, or thought leadership are not something that you can just claim. Take humility, for example. Imagine someone's reaction if you were to say, "I am definitely the most humble person in the world!" Huh? Knowing that most buyers are natural skeptics and we sellers are ultimately going to be judged by our actions, it's safe to assume that some of the most desirable and intangible human qualities (like humility) must actually be demonstrated in order to register value in the eyes of prospective clients.

An employment interview provides a good example of what I'm talking about. In fact, this is a metaphor that will be discussed at length throughout the book, not only because it provides a perfect backdrop to examine the interpersonal dynamics between buyers and sellers, but also because it provides a wonderful illustration for what it takes to sell in an environment where you are completely responsible for selling yourself.

Think about it like this. What's the value of a job interview?

Why would a company even bother to meet with potential candidates? Believe me, it's not just to review their work history or technical qualifications. The hiring manager can glean most of that right off your resume or from talking with references. The real value of a job interview is to allow both parties a chance to actually get a *feel* for each other. Everyone looks good on paper. But once you bring human chemistry into the mix, the intangibles that each candidate brings to the table tend to separate people pretty quickly. In person, a hiring manager can see if you're attentive, enthusiastic, assertive, even humble. The real purpose of a job interview, therefore, is to evaluate important intangibles that otherwise wouldn't show up as specific line items on the candidate's resume.

> "Every job interview is a sales call, and every sales call is also a job interview."

The purpose of a sales conversation is similar. For customers, it's a chance to evaluate the vendor's value proposition; and for the salesperson, it's an opportunity to separate yourself from the rest of the noise in the marketplace. But again, the customer's perception of value often comes down to those same intangible qualities like integrity, leadership, helpfulness, vision, thoughtfulness, and credibility. Think of it this way. Every job interview is a sales call, and every sales call is also a job interview.

So, what does it really mean to be forthright and honest? Given my newfound affection for *The Wizard of Oz*, it would be easy for me in a sales situation to say, "Mr. Customer, would it be valuable for me to pull back the curtains and show you what's really important for customers who are making this type of decision?" Gosh, you might even be accused of sounding straightforward and down-to-earth by saying this to one of your customers. Don't you think this type of interaction would be valuable to decision makers in today's business environment?

The twist comes when you introduce the element of time into the mix. Given enough time, customers would surely come to recognize the value of your products, and once they got to know you personally, they would undoubtedly appreciate your value-add as well. But, sellers aren't always afforded endless amounts of time with prospective customers. Thus, to be effective, salespeople must start thinking about how to accomplish your sales goals in the small windows of opportunity you get with decision makers and key influencers. You also need to think in terms of gaining as much traction as possible with potential clients, because in a ten minute sales call or even an hour-long job interview, if the first part of your conversation doesn't go well, you may not get a second chance.

Given our desire to make the best use of the customer's time, we should be asking ourselves certain questions like, how can we establish more credibility earlier in our conversations with prospective customers? Or, how can we identify more needs in order to create a greater sense of urgency to move forward? How can we pique the customer's curiosity on a first time call and then grow their interest over time, and get deeper, wider, and more strategic within target accounts? How do we cause customers to recognize the intangible qualities we bring to the table, and then leverage those character traits to tip the scales and win the business when the sale would otherwise come down to a virtual tie between two or more competitors? Most importantly, how can you do all this within the brief windows of time you get to spend with prospective and existing customers?

If you adopt the specific techniques outlined in this book, and focus on what is now required to be effective in terms of selling yourself, you will engage customers in more in-depth and more productive conversations than you ever thought possible. During turbulent times, buyers do tend to tighten their belts and it's likely that hungry salespeople will be competing more and more aggressively for increasingly elusive pieces of the economic pie. I can assure you, however, that whether you are interviewing for a job or negotiating a product sale, commerce will continue long into the foreseeable future and people will be taking advice and buying solutions from somebody. That leaves the question, to what extent are customers going to choose to deal with you?

Imagine how cool it would be if your response to the perfect storm of today's competitive business environment was to create a perfect win-win-win scenario, where the salesperson, your company, and the customer all benefited by your newfound ability to stay ahead of this rapidly changing marketplace. Given that sellers now stand to either gain or lose marketshare in their respective industries, this is definitely the time to start thinking about how to more effectively differentiate yourself in the short term, and into the foreseeable future.

Chapter 2

Your Next Job Interview

Professionals are constantly enhancing their resumes in continuous preparation for their next job opportunity. Even if you stay with the same company, you will likely change positions, either by moving into a new role or by being next in line for a big promotion.

Ironically, a job interview scenario provides the perfect metaphor for selling yourself in today's competitive marketplace. Even if you are indeed the most valuable candidate applying for a position, you still have to say and do things during a job interview (or sales call) that will enable you to be perceived as such.

Make no mistake, a job interview is definitely a *sales* situation. Although my primary objective in this book isn't to encourage you or anyone else to change jobs, the interview scenario is one to which virtually everyone can relate. Whether you are being considered for a new position within your current organization or you are pursuing a fresh start with a new company, you will be competing with other qualified applicants who are also vying for the same desirable position. In those scenarios, you will undoubtedly be responsible for selling yourself.

The realization that your performance during a job interview will have a direct impact on the outcome of the manager's hiring decision can be frightening and empowering at the same time. If the meeting goes well, you certainly have the right to congratulate yourself for a good showing. A successful interview is a wonderful confidence builder. On the other hand, knowing that any missteps during the interview process could threaten your chances can be very intimidating. Either way, your success during an employment interview is largely dependent on you, and more importantly, how you are being perceived by the person sitting across the desk.

Why am I talking about how to handle yourself during a job interview? Frankly, an employment interview is probably the closest you will ever come to actually *selling yourself*. In these situations, the hiring manager becomes the customer, and you, in effect, are the salesperson. The interview itself then transforms into a classic Sales 101 scenario, where the host company is attempting to fill a certain position and your goal is to impress the hiring manager enough to convince him or her that your talent, experience, and abilities would provide the best solution. During a job interview, you are essentially the product that's being offered and the interviewer is, first and foremost, deciding whether or not to buy into *you*.

> "Your success during an employment interview or sales call is largely dependent on how you are perceived by the person sitting across the desk."

Whether you are competing for your first career opportunity out of school or you are hoping to secure a big promotion with your current company, applying sound sales logic to your next job interview gives you a strategic advantage over everyone else. Most candidates will simply default to what I would refer to as an old-school or classic approach to selling themselves. If you are strategic, however, and you understand how to position yourself in a way that differentiates you from other candidates, you will maximize your probability of success not only to secure the desired job opportunity, but also to exceed your sales goals in today's competitive marketplace.

You may have heard the axiom, "Everybody sells all the time!" Well, it's true. Most people are selling themselves every day in some fashion. Whether you hold a traditional sales job or you are in a customer support role, if you interact with customers in any capacity, the customer's perception of your company and products will be impacted by the impression they end up forming about you. Consequently, in my simple way of thinking, *you* are selling yourself every day—to customers, partners, colleagues, your employer, and even to friends and family when you are not at work.

The whole notion of *Selling Yourself* is a culmination of the overall communication philosophy that I have been advocating and teaching for many years. My premise for this book is pretty simple and straightforward. One of the most important reasons people would want to buy from you, hire you, or deal with you at all, is because of *you*! At the end of the day, *you* are the one who will invest the time to understand the customer's needs and *you* will educate them as to how your offerings compare to other options being considered. *You* may also be in the best position to suggest solution alternatives that will help decision makers achieve both their business and personal objectives. No matter what job title you have in your current company, or what role you might be interviewing for, the unique blend of knowledge, experience, and insight that *you* bring to the table makes you a potentially valuable resource and an integral part of the overall solution.

The fact that salespeople directly contribute to their own success is a double-edged sword, however. When everything goes well, popping corks and cheers of congratulations can be heard for miles around. There's a sobering flipside to this reality. If for some reason you are not getting the results you desire, then it's possible that you may need to look inward to identify the culprit.

Frankly, I have been training professionals long enough to know that most people don't relish the idea of being on the receiving end of constructive feedback. Don't worry, my goal here is not to ruffle anyone's feathers, point fingers, or attempt to indict the sales establishment. Most of the salespeople I've worked with over the years are honest, caring, hard-working people. But, if you are truly motivated by success and are willing to take an objective look at yourself through the eyes of others, I think you will discover that there is a significant upside opportunity to provide even greater value to customers by adjusting the way you position yourself.

Ask yourself, are you the type of individual people can trust? Do colleagues and customers solicit your input and opinions? Are you intelligent, beyond just being knowledgeable about your industry? Do you have the customer's best interests at heart when offering advice? Let's assume for a moment that your answer to these questions is a resounding yes. Great, but how are customers supposed to know you are all these things?

I'm sure your good friends and best customers already recognize your value. But, what about new people you meet? You have to believe that every seller who walks through the customer's door, and every candidate who comes into the hiring manager's office claims to be the best. Unfortunately, all the 'chest pounding' in the world doesn't change the fact that just because someone claims to be great, doesn't necessarily make it so.

During an employment interview, what will differentiate you from the previous candidate who was quietly ushered out of the hiring manager's office just minutes before you arrived? Or, during a sales call, what separates you from the seven or eight other salespeople who previously called on the customer and delivered a "sounds too good to be true" sales pitch?

A fair amount of skepticism now exists in the marketplace where customers have become increasingly standoffish toward sellers they don't yet know or trust. Believe me when I tell you that this trend is not going to reverse itself anytime soon. Let's not blame the customer. You and I are just as reticent to share information with those pesky sellers who call us at home during dinner. Contrary to popular belief, most customers don't actually despise salespeople. In fact, most customers depend on salespeople—as a source for information, ideas, a vision into the future, and for solutions. They

> "Most customers depend on salespeople as a source for information, for ideas, a vision into the future and solutions."

just don't depend on *all* of them. So, out of all the sellers calling the same target customers, some small fraction of those vendor representatives are going to be seen as valuable resources. The question now is, how consistently are you being included in that small fraction of people who are perceived to be of value? Or, if you buy into my premise that you contribute to your own success, perhaps I should pose the question a different way: How consistently are you "putting yourself" in the customer's select group of chosen vendors?

That's enough high-level sales philosophy. What salespeople really want is a system—a repeatable formula that can be implemented and managed, that will produce a noticeable positive result. My approach to selling is based almost entirely on a mutually beneficial coexistence between buyers and sellers and the cause and effect interactions that will ultimately impact your relationships. Simply put, people do buy from people, and the extent to which someone will put their trust in you or accept your advice has a lot to do with your approach. Hence, most of our attention throughout this book is focused on two things— *your* approach to selling yourself and how you can impact the customer's perception of *your* value.

As you implement the techniques and strategies we discuss, you will discover numerous ways to enhance your credibility in the eyes of potential customers and raise the level of respect and confidence they express toward you as a trusted advisor. Furthermore, I am very pleased to see that more attention is finally being given to the softer skills of selling yourself, which I believe has been the missing ingredient in traditional business theory for many years, and is a refreshing change from cumbersome process models. You will find that the logic behind the idea of selling yourself is also the common thread among highly effective sales producers, and this same logic will be the catalyst that propels you to attain top performer status at your company, and within your industry.

The Biggest Difference is You

Success in selling is ultimately about customer perception—specifically, the customer's perception of the value you offer. If the value of your product or service is perceived by customers as greater than a competitor's offering, then you are in a strong position to differentiate yourself and possibly even command a premium price. On the other hand, if your product or service is perceived to be less valuable than similarly positioned alternatives, the reverse is true and you will likely be facing a significant competitive disadvantage.

The sales and marketing world has struggled for years to get its 'intellectual arms' around is this notion of perceived value. Millions of corporate dollars have been spent on initiatives to gain a competitive advantage with respect to product placement, promotional advertising, sponsorships, brand recognition, data mining, and demographics. As much or more resources have been poured into diagnosing consumer behavior and identifying "why" they buy. Still, the number one issue facing most organizations remains the same—how to duplicate the success of top performing salespeople. In every company, some salespeople are clearly more successful than others, even though they are basically offering the same menu of products to the same types of customers.

One might wonder why cracking the code on the secret to this sales formula has eluded our focus for so long. Back when I was a neophyte salesperson, I vividly remember wondering what it was that top performing salespeople were doing that I wasn't. What gave them such a competitive edge?

Some people say you have to be a born salesperson. From

my perspective, it's a bit of a cop-out to attribute high perform-ance to inherent character traits like personal charm, charisma, personality, or just having superior DNA. Frankly, I've met plenty of charming people who are now struggling mightily in this new economy to meet their sales goals. On the other hand, I have also met some pretty successful sales nerds over the years—if you can call someone a "nerd" whose success now has them flying around in a private jet.

I agree that some people are naturally endowed with certain innate gifts. But, if you attribute consistent high performance with things that are totally out of your control, you will prob-ably never realize your full potential in sales. As evidence of this, during the 1980's, I fell short of my sales quota during my first few years in corporate sales. As time marched on, and I became increasingly more frustrated with missing my sales goals, I started making adjustments to my approach. Within a short time after I started doing things differently, I dramatically exceeded my sales numbers to finish over two-hundred percent of quota for multiple consecutive years. During that period, my DNA remained the same, and I was no more or less charming, but my approach to selling myself changed dramatically. So did my perspective on being successful in life.

In competitive sales situations, the difference between your proposal and a competitor's offering can often be very small, if not negligible. It is possible to have a unique offering, where your product or service does something that customers must have and no one else can provide. It's more often the case in a competitive market that you don't have an exclusive offering, and there are other vendors who can offer similarly viable solutions.

In the case of pursuing a career opportunity, chances are

good that you will be competing against other applicants who will present a resume that is equally impressive to yours. Yet, decision makers and hiring managers are quick to form opinions, and they will generally exhibit a clear preference for one candidate (or vendor) over another. When pressed, these decision makers may cite various reasons to support their impressions, but if you listen carefully, there is no clear cut differentiator in most cases. Instead, you will hear hiring managers say, "I just felt more comfortable with this person," or, "I thought we clicked." It wasn't the product, the company, or the resume that created the biggest differentiation; rather, it was the intangible qualities of the way your product or offering was being represented to the customer. This has everything to do with how you position yourself, and ultimately, how you are being perceived.

If we agree that selling yourself in today's competitive marketplace is directly linked to your overall effectiveness and future success, then please excuse my candor as I drop a bombshell that may change your perspective on selling forever. What do you think would happen if we discovered that how most salespeople have been taught to communicate value is literally upside-down from how customers make decisions?

> "How most salespeople have been taught to sell is literally up-side-down from how most customers make decisions."

Seriously, what if you found out that the traditional approach to selling was actually backwards from how most people process information or make purchase decisions? Trying to leverage an approach that is literally upside-down and backwards doesn't make sense. The good news is, recognizing this discrepancy creates a significant upside opportunity for those salespeople willing to adjust their strategy.

The most effective way that I have found to show people how to reposition and enhance their value proposition is to explore more specifically what happens when you are actually selling yourself—in the case of an employment interview. This metaphor is not only legitimate advice for someone hunting for a new opportunity in a competitive job market, it's also the best way to show sellers how to increase their current sales volume.

Meeting the New Boss

Picture yourself walking into your next job interview. You're on time, and you can feel an involuntary surge of nervous energy pumping through your veins. With a slightly clammy palm, you reach out and shake the outstretched hand of your potential new boss. "It's nice to meet you," you say, intentionally trying speak clearly so as not to bumble the introduction.

Everyone knows that it's important to make a good first impression. Particularly in a business setting, when you are meeting someone for the first time, you obviously want to start off on the right foot. If you have a knack for sizing people up, or you have the presence of mind to scan the room for subtle clues, you might get a feel for the hiring manager's personality and disposition. It doesn't take a rocket scientist to tell whether the person you are meeting is having a bad day or feeling pushed for time. So, you put on a happy face and walk into the office, keenly aware that they are sizing you up, too, and forming their first impressions at the same time.

I'm not a fan of gimmicky interviews, like when the interviewer makes an applicant sit in an uncomfortable chair or presents them with awkward questions to see how they handle themselves. Most of these interviewing tactics went out of vogue with the previous generation of chauvinistic bosses. Honestly, if you do encounter a disrespectful interviewer, you might want to think twice about whether you really want to work for that company. Fortunately, most hiring managers don't play games with potential new-hires, so we won't waste a lot of time dealing with interviewing tricks.

The purpose of a job interview is generally pretty clear. It is an opportunity to meet with qualified candidates in order to evaluate their skills relative to the needs of an open position within the company. Since multiple candidates are usually being considered, hiring managers will document the information gleaned during the various interviews, assess their alternatives, and ultimately select the person who presumably provides the best fit from the pool of applicants. As we said before, the actual hiring decision is based largely on impressions that get formed during these interviews. Can you see why the metaphor of selling yourself is so fitting? Mind you, the interviewer and candidate both play an important role in these meetings. As in any legitimate transaction, an employment opportunity should be mutually beneficial and meet the needs of both the hiring manager and the applicant.

A certain amount of casual chit-chat or small talk is a common starting point for most job interviews. Hiring managers want to observe you at your best. So, they want qualified candidates to feel comfortable and relaxed. They might ask, "How was your trip across town?" Or, "Were the directions helpful?" Or, "How is your summer going?" But, after some brief light-hearted banter, the conversation will quickly transition to the purpose at hand—the actual job interview.

Let me back up a little and say, just as any good salesperson would diligently prepare prior to meeting important customers, you should definitely prepare for an important interview. Hopefully, you would have done some research on the company, its product offerings, and its financial status in advance. Perhaps you've even typed the interviewer's name into your favorite search engine. It's also good to have a list of questions in mind that you would like to ask the interviewer about the company and the specific job opportunity.

In anticipation of the meeting, candidates strategize (and worry) about the types of questions that might get asked during the interview and how best to answer. There's no need to wonder what the first question will be during an employment interview, however, as the opening salvo from virtually every hiring manager is the same. At the appropriate time in the discourse, the hiring manager will say something to the effect of, "So, why don't you tell me a little about yourself?"

Now it's just a matter of answering the question, right? Perhaps, but let's not miss the target completely on your very first shot. Although there are a couple ways to respond to this initial interview question, I can tell you without a doubt that the standard answer most interviewees give is *not* the most effective response. Do you remember what I said about the traditional approach to selling being upside-down from how most customers think? Let me further the metaphor to illustrate.

What's Most Important to the Customer?

When this proverbial first softball question gets tossed out by the hiring manager, "Tell me a little about yourself," most people respond by doing just that—they tell about themselves. Hmmm. Is that wrong? One wouldn't necessarily think so, since that's what the interviewer seems to be inviting the candidate to do. But, there's always more than one way to skin a cat and the best way to respond to this question (from a customer's perspective) might have less to do with you, and more to do with those things which are most important to them.

If you think about a job interview as a sales situation, a candidate who wants to secure a desirable position with a quality company would definitely be trying to sell himself or herself to the hiring manager. These roles can sometimes be reversed if a hiring manager is trying to attract top-notch recruits into the company. But, for all practical purposes, in your next interview, you will be selling yourself to the hiring manager.

Once we have a firm grasp on who is selling to whom, let's ask ourselves this question: What's more important to the typical buyer—their own goals, issues and concerns or a salesperson's objectives? This may seem like a rhetorical question, since most customers are clearly more focused on their own goals and objectives than they are interested in hearing a product pitch.

To prove the point, suppose you came down with a bad case of spring fever, which brought on a sudden urge to purchase a new automobile. Or, maybe you decide that your expanding business needed an additional set of wheels. Or, on a whim, perhaps you just wanted to upgrade your current ride to a new model. So, you head off to one of the local dealerships to do some car shopping. Before you've even had a chance to step all the way out of your vehicle at the first dealership, a typical car salesman scurries over and introduces himself. With an outstretched hand and a hundred dollar smile, he says, "How can I help you today?"

At that moment, what do you suppose is most important to the typical customer, their specific car-hunting objectives or the salesperson's career aspirations? I think we already know the answer. Let's play out the dialogue.

Car Salesman: *"How can I help you today?"*

Customer: *"I'd like to explore some options for purchasing a new vehicle."*

Car Salesman: *"Well, Sir, you've come to the right place. Southern Motors has a track record of customer service dating all the way back to when my grandfather started the business fifty years ago.*

Yes, sir, we pride ourselves on delivering the most bang for the buck. In addition to our fabulous showroom filled with brand new automobiles, we also boast the largest inventory of used cars and trucks in the area. If for some reason you don't see what you're looking for on the lot, our crack team of vehicle locaters will find one that you are sure to like. Our finance department also offers comprehensive terms for leased and purchased vehicles with the best rates in town!"

Whew! I'm already tired of car shopping. Aren't you? If this had been the second or third car dealership you visited so far today, wouldn't this pitch sound just like the others? While the salesman's opening litany probably contains some useful information, I can assure you that the typical customer is much more interested in their own goals, objectives, problems, issues, needs, wants and desires, than they are in hearing a sales pitch. At some point, this particular car salesperson might be better advised to find out some basic information—like if the desired vehicle is going to be for personal use or strictly business. It might also be helpful to find out whether the customer is leaning toward buying a sedan, sport utility vehicle, van, or light truck. Most customers have at least a couple of specs in mind when they start out on this type of quest, don't you think?

During an employment interview, hiring managers usually have specific objectives in mind as well, including short and long term objectives they would like to accomplish by hiring the right person. Whether they are trying to replace an employee who recently left the company or are populating a new team for a start-up division, the manager is probably looking for a certain skill profile, in addition to finding a good cultural fit. Personal preferences, style, and priorities will vary between interviewers, and qualified candidates are not always privy to the underlying nuances that may be driving the hiring manager's decision. But one thing's for sure. Goal-oriented managers are looking for people who can help them and the company to accomplish 'their' specific goals. Therefore, it's safe to assume that the candidate who is perceived to be most likely to help the decision maker accomplish his or her objectives has the best shot at being offered the position.

Again, even if you are the most selfless, customer-focused

person in the world, you still must be perceived as such—particularly early in the decision process when customers (in this case, the hiring manager) are forming their initial impressions. The question now becomes, during your next formal job interview, sales call, or sales situation of any kind, what impression do you want the hiring manager (or customer) to form about you?

Knowing What the Competition Sounds Like

Week after week during our QBS training seminars, I concoct pretend job interview scenarios to illustrate this point. In doing so, I invite a few audience members to role play with me as a way to see how they currently position themselves to customers. It turns out that the approach most people use during a job interview best mirrors the approach they are also likely to gravitate to when selling their products and services. Given our premise throughout the book that *you* are the biggest differentiator in the sales process, this exercise points out just how easy it is to sound like every *Tom*, *Dick*, or *Harry* who is similarly trying to sell themselves while competing for the same opportunities.

In this role play, I select a volunteer from the audience and then I assume the role of the hiring manager. To emulate the typical exchange, I initiate the dialogue by simply saying, "Tell me a little about yourself." Here's a sample of how the exchange usually plays out, after the initial small talk.

Manager: *"Thank you for coming to interview with us today. Why don't you tell me a little about yourself?"*

Candidate: *"Well, I have been with my current company for the past five years in a variety of roles, most recently as sales and marketing liaison for the largest implementation of our product in North America. Prior to that, I was an account manager in Chicago for three years, and I also completed the management training program out of our corporate headquarters in Philadelphia.*

While an account manager, I achieved my sales quota two out of three years, and made President's Club both times.

I graduated from the local university in 1997. After college, I went to work in the family business, which was sold four years later. I thought about going back for my MBA, but that's about the time when my wife and I started having children. We now have two kids, a boy who just turned six and a new baby girl. Consequently, I was hoping to find an opportunity that would allow me to make more money and spend time with my family.

I am willing to travel, but not too much, and I would like to have flexibility for choosing vacation days.

My salary requirements are...blah, blah, blah..."

Let me interrupt this reenactment for a moment. The person being interviewed is responding exactly as requested—he's telling the hiring manager 'a little' about himself. On the surface, the candidate seems like a decent person as far as we can tell from this short excerpt. But, something is clearly missing from this sample dialogue.

In a classroom setting, I often invite a second or third person to partake in the same exercise as a way to establish a baseline for what the 'standard approach' to a job interview usually sounds like. Once the audience hears two or three people respond to the interviewer's initial question in pretty much the same manner, by telling about themselves, we quickly realize that the typical approach is probably very similar to what your competition also says during their job interviews. Still, something is definitely missing.

Virtually everyone who participates in this exercise responds the same way—they rattle off a litany of bullet points summarizing their personal history, which I assume is an attempt to position themselves in the best light. What's missing is any mention of, or concern for, what the hiring manager's goals or objectives might be. If you notice, our candidate in the sample dialogue is totally consumed with his own work history, current situation, and personal desires. It's fine to have goals and to express them, but you must recognize that customers also have goals, and to them, their goals are far more important than yours. Frankly, this scenario we've outlined where the person describes themselves ad nauseum may well be a characterization of how *not* to begin a job interview or sales call. By the time the hiring manager has seen two or three qualified candidates, the specific details from each interview will all start to blend and potentially be forgotten as the candidates' personal backgrounds all mush together.

One of the reasons *your next job interview* provides such a great metaphor for selling is that the same thing often happens to prospective customers when they evaluate multiple vendors.

After a while, all the claims of market leadership and product superiority start to blend together, to the point where customers start to forget who said what. What happens then? A confused customer could choose to delay the decision. An overwhelmed customer might decide not to move forward at all. A customer who doesn't fully understand the differences between the options might just flip a coin or choose the vendor who offers the lowest price.

This need to differentiate yourself dictates that sellers must do something to stand out in the customer's mind. So, let me ask: What specifically are you doing to set yourself apart from the competition? In fact, if your approach is causing you to sound the same as everyone else, then you forfeit any competitive advantages. Believe me, you don't want your next job interview or sales opportunity to come down to a coin flip.

Fortunately for those who are striving to differentiate themselves, there is another tack to take that will instantly set you apart from the rest of the masses. Let me show you what I mean.

What a Hiring Manager Really Wants

Let's not over think this. When a manager interviews potential candidates for an open position, he is undoubtedly trying to address one or more specific business goals by hiring the right person. That's not selfish or self-serving. It's only logical that the customer wants to select the person or product who can help them the most. Keep in mind that we do the same thing when we're the customer. We evaluate our options and then make a decision based on the solution that seems best for us at the time.

Therefore, if we shift our focus and consider for a moment

what the customer's needs might be, what business objectives do you suppose the hiring manager at your next job interview might want to address? It's difficult to know exactly, but if we put together a top ten list of desirable attributes for the perfect candidate, I bet it would include some of the following:

Desirable Qualities Sought by Interviewer
1. Knowledge, experience, savvy.
2. Likeable, easy to get along with.
3. Customer-focused.
4. Blend with current business culture.
5. Quick learner, short ramp-up time.
6. Offer a fresh perspective, new ideas.
7. Independent, motivated, self-starter.
8. Track record of success.
9. Positive attitude.
10. Solid references.

Can we agree that if a new employee possessed each and every one of these attributes, they would be a pretty good hire and potentially a valuable long-term asset for the company? The challenge for candidates is, how do you convey that you indeed possess these qualities, more so than other candidates competing for the same position? You could get on your soapbox during the interview and claim to be a quick learner who is smart, likable, independent, motivated, and a self-starter. Did I forget humble? Trying to articulate one's own strengths during a job interview or sales call always poses a challenge for candidates and salespeople because there's a fine line between seeming confident, and sounding pompous or arrogant.

Alas, we come to a crossroads in selling philosophy where you must now choose between traditional sales thinking and a differentiation strategy that will elevate your game to the next level. The first step toward implementation is simple. Just ask yourself this question: What's more important to most decision makers, focusing on a salesperson's personal agenda or accomplishing their own specific goals and objectives? If you believe, as I do, that being customer-focused is the correct answer, then it may be time to make some adjustments to your approach.

The Customer-Focused Alternative

My philosophy on the best way to position yourself during a job interview or on a sales call is pretty straightforward. Figure out what the customer wants or needs and then gear the entire conversation toward that. This includes demonstrating that you are indeed customer-focused from the moment you meet the hiring manager, as opposed to trying to dig yourself out of a hole later on in the conversation.

In the case of a job interview, it's actually quite easy. Just think about what *you* would want (or need) if roles were reversed. Zig Ziglar, my all-time favorite motivational speaker used to say, "The best way to get what you want...is to help enough other people get what they want." He was right. Let's see what happens if we apply this logic to our interview scenario.

Manager: *"Dale, thanks for meeting with me today. Can you tell me a little about yourself?"*

Candidate: *"Sure. Do you have a copy of my resume?*

Manager: *"Yes, I've got it right here."*

Candidate: *"Well, since you have a snapshot of my work history already, I'll just add that I think I'm a good person, a hard worker, and have a decent track record for success, but my guess is you may be looking for more than that to fill this position—perhaps some of the intangibles that don't always show up as specific line items on a resume.*

For example, I'm guessing that in addition to finding someone with knowledge and experience, you might be looking for someone who could ramp up and become productive as quickly as possible. You might also want a person who can blend well with the current culture, but who could also contribute new ideas and possibly provide a fresh perspective. You may also be looking for someone with a positive attitude, who is self-motivated and customer-focused. Am I close?"

Manager: *"Absolutely."*

Candidate: *"Well, those are the types of things that have enabled me to be successful thus far, and that's what I would bring to the table in this position as well."*

You're hired! The interviewer would literally be jumping up and down in their chair if the first impression they formed was, "Wow, this person really understands the type of person I'm looking for!"

Notice in the dialogue that the candidate's response allows him to tell about himself, but in the context of goals and issues that would likely be most important to the customer. That's very different from just launching into a diatribe about yourself. You don't even have to claim that you are extraordinarily equipped in all of these areas. The pure fact that you are preemptive in raising these issues says a lot about your strategic thought process and your potential value to an organization.

Be aware that your success in a formal job interview (or sales call) is not just about the initial impression that gets formed. There will be plenty of opportunities to talk about yourself and your solutions as the discussion unfolds, and I will lay out the entire strategy for *Positioning Your Solutions* later in Chapter 9. For now, let's just acknowledge that the first impression someone forms about you or your offering sets the tone for the rest of the meeting. If you are able to get the meeting off to a good start, there will be plenty of opportunities to have more in-depth conversation about your qualifications and how they match up to the opportunity being evaluated.

One important note. Our intent here is not to trick or fool the interviewer, or to dodge the interviewer's initial question. There's nothing covert or manipulative about focusing on those things that are most important to your customers. However, we should be mindful of the fact that a job interview is a competitive situation, and we absolutely do want to 'wow' the hiring manager in a way that differentiates us from the other candidates being considered.

Making this one small adjustment is relatively easy. Just remember to focus on whatever happens to be most important to the customer—their goals, objectives, needs, wants, desires, problems, issues, and concerns. Customers are focused on their own needs first and foremost. That's why the idea of selling yourself has to be about understanding what's important to the customer (first), in order for them to perceive maximum value from the attributes you bring to the table.

Of course, the more goals, objectives, needs, wants, desires, problems, issues, and concerns you are able to identify and address, the more opportunities you will have to provide value to potential customers. This raises another question. How can a salesperson or job applicant know what's most important to prospects that you are meeting for the very first time?

That's what we'll talk about next.

Chapter 3

Customers Won't Trust
Just Anyone

Have you ever been 'burned' by a salesperson? Most people have somewhere along the way. When it happens, decision makers become even more cautious toward other vendors, which makes the next salesperson's task of earning trust an even bigger challenge.

Selling solutions is fine. But, if you want to build strong customer relationships, you must first address the decision maker's most important concern, which is knowing who to trust.

A handsome, well-dressed representative from ABC Corp. confidently steps up and says to a potential customer, "Buy from us, we're the industry leader!" A few hours later, a salesperson from a different vendor shows up saying, "Buy from us, we offer the highest level of service and our track record is undeniably the best!" Meanwhile, a third vendor has an appointment to stop by later this afternoon and you already know they're going to say, "Choose us, we're number one!"

One could say customers have a much easier choice when multiple vendors are competing for their business, especially when the products being offered are very similar. Just pick your favorite supplier, or the one who offers the lowest price, and place the order. If for some reason the chosen vendor stumbles or fails to meet expectations, the customer can easily switch horses and call someone else to provide basically the same thing.

But, what happens when the options being considered are not functionally equivalent, and the customer must make a not-so-obvious choice between proposed solutions that aren't exactly the same? Whether a corporation is buying a database for a large-scale IT implementation or an elderly couple sits down at the kitchen table to evaluate supplemental health insurance, customers face the daunting task of sifting through all kinds of market literature and sales hype to somehow select the best alternative. What's the best way to compare apples and oranges? The decision is further complicated by the fact that every vendor in the mix claims to offer the best solution.

Each of the salespeople who presents a proposal will predictably don a polished smile and be well-versed in exchanging pleasantries at the beginning of the conversation. Knowing that the ramifications of making a bad decision can be costly or even irreversible, how are diligent customers supposed to know which vendor or proposal to choose? The answer, along with the outcome of the sale, will largely depend on which salesperson the customer chooses to trust.

The Foundation for All Relationships

If the intangible nature of *perceived value* is sometimes difficult for customers to quantify, try putting a fence around the notion of *trust*. Let me ask this question: Who is it that you trust? I bet it's not some cold-caller on the telephone who's offering a fantastic deal chosen "just for you!" They are presumably trying to sell you the ideal solution, and they don't even know you. It's important to realize that some of your prospective customers may be just as reticent to engage in an open dialogue when meeting you for the first time.

There's no doubt that our business culture has grown increasingly more cautious toward vendors. I'm not trying to make a political statement with this assertion. I am simply the messenger conveying a widely accepted observation that our society has become much less trusting when it comes to engaging someone with whom we do not already have an established relationship. It stands to reason that getting burned or being disappointed by one vendor's actions could very easily cause customers to lose faith in the system, making it that much more difficult for the next salesperson who comes calling to build a trusting relationship. You could even say that the general lack of trust has evolved to the point where I recently saw a bumper sticker in a church parking lot that read, "Trust in God, but lock your car!"

Understanding the dynamics of how mutual trust is created is particularly important for salespeople these days because trust serves as the foundation for building solid relationships, whether personal or professional. If someone is not willing to trust you, it is unlikely that any attempts you make at forging a relationship with them will ever get off the ground. Trust is also a critical element for maintaining existing relationships. At the point where someone decides they can no longer trust you, whatever relationship you may have had with them will abruptly come to an end.

Once we agree that trust is the foundation of every relationship, it's important to note that trust comes in different forms. In terms of interpersonal relations, trust can officially be defined as *having a firm reliance on the integrity, ability, or character of a person or thing.* For example, I trust my wife implicitly and my two daughters most of the time. I also trust that our clients will pay their invoices on time. I even trust that there will be a rental car and hotel room waiting for me when I arrive at my next destination, provided I booked a reservation in advance. Although the sentiment being conveyed by the word trust is always context dependent, the emotion is still highly intangible. Trust isn't something you hold in your hand or measure empirically, but you can definitely sense whether someone trusts you or not.

> "Trust is a long term human emotion that grows out of the confidence one develops from successive encounters where the other person's expectations were met or exceeded."

What are the chances that customers will implicitly trust the very next person who walks through their door or calls them on the telephone? If it's a salesperson they are meeting for the first time, the chances are slim. To date, I haven't discovered any magic button that can be pushed to cause someone to trust you instantaneously. Some folks might be willing to give you the benefit of the doubt, but let's not confuse common courtesy with an inherent level of trust. Trust is a long term human emotion that grows out of the confidence one develops from successive encounters where the other person's expectations were either met or exceeded. As I'm sure most of us know, you can lose someone's trust in an instant, but it takes a series of positive affirmations to earn it over time.

Contrary to popular belief, however, trust is *not* a good strategic target for salespeople to aim at when trying to forge new relationships with potential customers. Of course, you want customers to trust you. And, if you constantly meet and exceed their expectations, they will begin to trust you at some point. But, just as you wouldn't truly trust someone after spending a few minutes with them during a job interview, it's impossible to cause new prospects to implicitly "trust" you after a single telephone call. Instead, you are better served in today's selling environment to focus your efforts on the concept of establishing credibility.

While it can take some time to truly earn someone's trust, a savvy salesperson can begin to establish credibility with prospective customers almost immediately if they have the right strategy. Fortunately for us sellers, the concepts of credibility and trust are interrelated. As you earn more and more credibility with customers over time, they will absolutely begin to trust you.

The trick is having a repeatable method that enables you to establish as much credibility as possible, early in your sales conversations, thereby giving you get maximum "traction" with potential customers when forging new relationships. The rest of this chapter is a lesson in how to accomplish that.

Solution, Problem, Alternative (The SPA Approach)

Another key question I like to ask sales professionals is: How do customers know you're smart? Surely, everyone is aware that some salespeople are more knowledgeable, or have more experience, or are simply more capable, than others. So, how does a potential customer, meeting you for the very first time, know how *you* stack up? Do you pitch them on the value of your solutions hoping that product features will differentiate you from other salespeople? Or, do you just tell them how smart and wonderful you are and accept the risk that self-aggrandizing could come off sounding arrogant or presumptuous?

Unfortunately, it has become natural for salespeople to rely on self-promotion—telling about themselves or their products in the hopes of verbalizing enough value to touch a nerve or pique the interest of prospective buyers. Do you remember the job interview verbiage from Chapter 2? It really is amazing how quickly job applicants (salespeople) will break into a litany about themselves or their offerings when given the opportunity. I suppose that's just a reflection of how our selling culture has evolved over the years.

Case in point, companies invest millions of marketing dollars every year to generate stronger and more impactful market messages that they can distribute to their field sales organizations in the hopes of gaining a competitive advantage. When those same companies hire me, one of the first things I do is inject a dose of reality into the mix, pointing out that the traditional strategy of opening with an 'elevator pitch' about the company or product actually puts a salesperson or sales organization in an extremely weak position.

> "Opening with an 'elevator pitch' about the company or product puts a salesperson in an extremely weak position."

You see, back in the 1980's and early 1990's, a paradigm

shift occurred in the marketplace, where sales leaders began to recognize that it was more lucrative to focus on selling the total solution as opposed to just selling product features. As a result, sales conversations began to shift from being product-centric to instead focusing on selling solutions, even though the company itself or the products being recommended hadn't really changed. Particularly in large accounts, proposing an entire suite of products and services provided fully integrated solutions for the customer and nice big fat commission checks for the seller. Solutions, solutions, solutions…it was all about selling solutions. Ever since, the word "solutions" has turned into the favorite lingual condiment of marketers everywhere, as it is regularly used to enrich the headlines on everything from corporate web pages to product literature.

Selling solutions continues to be a good business strategy in the current economic climate, although sellers must recognize that the game has changed once again. The focus of the sales conversation should no longer revolve around your solutions, as customers are much more interested in their own problems, issues, and concerns than they are in hearing a sales pitch.

Even so, sellers still gravitate naturally to an SPA approach when positioning themselves and their solutions. SPA is essentially how most salespeople have been conditioned by traditional sales models and also by their own experiences. Just like we saw with the employment interview metaphor, when a potential customer (hiring manager) says, "Tell me about yourself (your product)," we do exactly that. We start telling about our solutions (S), in the hopes of transitioning the conversation into a more in-depth discussion to uncover the customer's problems (P). Then, later in the sales process or dialogue, we fend off questions about how your product compares with other alternatives (A). We call this a traditional SPA approach.

I believe the reason most salespeople gravitate so naturally to SPA is because it's easier to talk about what we do know (our solutions) than what we don't necessarily know (the customer's problems). Maybe it's fortunate, however, that we've finally reached a point where the logic behind this idea of "selling solutions" can be called into question and more carefully examined. For example, let me point out a couple logic problems with the traditional SPA approach.

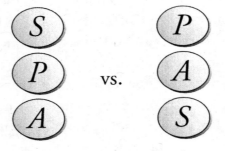

Again I must ask, what's more important to the typical customer when you first engage—their problems (P) or a salesperson's solutions (S)? From my vantage point, I believe that customers are much more focused on their own problems, goals, objectives, and needs than a salesperson's solutions. Therefore, it doesn't seem to make sense for a customer-focused salesperson to open his or her presentation with a data dump of product information (S) rather than focusing on the customer's problem (P).

Nonetheless, salespeople are quick to do this, as countless sales training classes are still being delivered that teach sellers to open with a perfunctory elevator pitch about their products. I'm sure some of you will think to yourselves, "I don't do that." And maybe you don't. But, to prove how prevalent SPA really is, you should try this experiment. Next time you deal with a salesperson of any kind, ask them, "Can you please tell me about your product?" At that moment, look at your watch and time how long they talk about themselves, their company, or their product before they realize that they have no idea what you might need, or even why you asked the question.

What's the alternative to SPA? Well, let's apply some deductive reasoning. In order to even have an opportunity to provide solutions, one must first be able to identify the customer's problem (P). We agreed earlier that it's important to be customer-focused, right? Well, if we know customers are much more interested in their own problems (P) than a salesperson's solutions (S), and we know that a salesperson must be able to identify a problem in order to provide valuable solutions, then wouldn't it make more sense to adjust your sales strategy to follow a PAS approach?

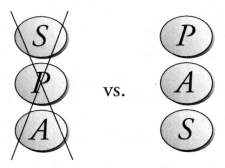

PAS is essentially the thought process most people use to make decisions. Not only is it how consumers decide whether or not to purchase a certain product or service, it's also how hiring managers assess and choose between multiple candidates interviewing for a new position.

Let me give you a perfect example. Have you purchased a digital camera in the last couple of years? If so, I'll try to guess at the thought process you probably used to make that decision—without knowing you personally. At some point you said to yourself, because I have this problem (a need to take great pictures on our upcoming vacation (P)), that the alternatives (my film camera, our movie camera, buying a disposable camera while on vacation, or taking no pictures at all (A)) don't solve as effectively, that's why I choose to buy a new digital camera (S).

Whether you are considering the purchase of a new computer, a car, a house, or a new outfit, the underlying decision process is essentially the same. In fact, I would argue that the same thought process applies to virtually all value-based decisions.

When a hospital administrator selects a supplier from which to purchase medical equipment, to win the business, the decision maker in the hospital must conclude the following. They must say to themselves, "Because we have certain goals, objectives, issues, concerns, wants, needs, desires, or problems (P), that the alternatives (other suppliers (A)) don't solve as effectively, that's why we choose to buy solutions (S) from this vendor.

The underlying logic of this thought process is actually quite simple—you bond with people on *their* goals, issues, concerns, needs, and problems (P), not your solutions (S). This especially makes sense in the selling arena because in order to communicate the value of your product or service, you must first have something to build value against. Bonding with customers on what is most important to them (their problems (P)) is also significant because that's what allows them to begin to trust you.

Avoid Rhetorical Questions

One of the most effective ways to earn credibility in a sales situation is to demonstrate high levels of capability and competence. Customers tend to bond with people they see as being knowledgeable, relevant, intelligent, and prepared, particularly if you come across as being extremely customer-focused. The best way to demonstrate competence is by asking relevant and intelligent questions, which we will talk about in much more depth later when we focus on needs development. For now, it's important to avoid falling into the trap of asking rhetorical questions to uncover customer needs.

The problem comes when a salesperson thinks to themselves, "I'm supposed to uncover the customer's needs, so I better start asking questions." Even though sales trainers have been beating this drum about asking questions for decades, there are some ineffective ways to ask questions that must be avoided. For example, it's not advisable to create a noticeable awkwardness at the beginning of your sales conversations by asking questions that are overly rhetorical.

If you were in a business that sells medical devices, high tech, financial services, or you were interviewing for a position with a company in one of those fields, then it's safe to assume you would have probably done some research prior to your actual sales call or employment interview. As a result of doing your homework in advance, I would argue that a capable and intelligent salesperson should know something about what customers *might* need before actually talking with them.

Prepping in advance for an important sales situation is probably a common practice for anyone who is reading this book. To illustrate the downside of asking rhetorical questions, however, let's revisit our previous interview scenario.

First impressions are important, correct? So, what do you suppose would happen if a job applicant responds to the interviewer's initial salvo by countering with a few probing questions to uncover the hiring manager's needs? Let's see.

Interviewer: *"Robert, thanks for coming to meet with us today. Can you tell me a little about yourself?"*

Candidate: *"What types of things would you be looking for in an employee?"*

Interviewer: *"Uh, well, I suppose we would like to select someone who is highly qualified and can grow in the position, and hopefully, with the company. What would you say are your best attributes?"*

Candidate: *"Are knowledge and experience important to you?"*

Interviewer: *(awkward silence)* *"Next!"*

While I appreciate that this applicant probably just wants to better understand the opportunity, the beginning of a sales situation is no time for playing games. From my perspective, when a customer asks you a question (in this case, the hiring manager), there is some obligation on the candidate's part to provide a meaningful response. Otherwise, you risk sounding like you are trying to dodge the interviewer's question. Don't worry, if the conversation gets off to a solid start, there will be plenty of chances for you to ask detailed questions about the opportunity, particularly if you demonstrate a level of competence early in the meeting and cause the person on the other side of the table to form a positive impression.

It's almost goofy that the candidate in this example responds to the interviewer's initial question by countering with a question of their own. Literally seconds into the interview, if I was the hiring manager, I would be wondering, "Why is this person avoiding my question?" "Has he not prepared in advance, or is he just playing games with me?" "Seriously, what does this candidate hope to accomplish by asking absurdly obvious questions, like asking if knowledge and experience are important?" Of course knowledge and experience are important!

If this candidate was hoping to impress the hiring manager or gather specific information about the opportunity, he has failed miserably on both counts. That's because asking rhetorical questions usually does not create a good first impression. Other than battling for control of the meeting, why would a capable job applicant or salesperson ask about something where the answer is totally obvious? If they had put any thought whatsoever into preparing for the meeting, they wouldn't ask such shallow-sounding questions.

Even worse, asking overly-rhetorical questions not only fails to breed confidence with potential buyers, it usually has the opposite effect. Picture the used car salesman who walks up to a prospective customer and asks, "Sir, is value important to you?" What's the customer going to say? "No, I was actually hoping to get ripped off." Of course, the customer wants a good value! Hence, asking questions that seem obvious or unnecessary is more likely to cause cautious customers to doubt your intentions, which will actually erode any credibility you may have had with them or were hoping to build.

I'm not suggesting that you should refrain from asking questions during a sales call or during your next job interview. The methodology I developed and have been teaching for over a decade is called Question Based Selling for a reason—because it has a lot to do with asking questions. But, you must be strategic with the types of questions you choose to ask, because we still face the reality that just because a salesperson wants to ask a bunch of questions doesn't change the fact that customers are not always open to sharing with someone they don't yet know or trust.

Striking a Chord of Connection

What you say and ask during a job interview, or any sales situation, is definitely important. But, your value in the eyes of your target audience is ultimately defined by how you are perceived. With that in mind, let's see what happens when we actually put this new PAS positioning logic into practice. Besides sounding very different from other candidates in the first few moments of the dialogue, taking a PAS approach is a sure-fire way to pique the hiring manager's interest and strike a chord of connection by raising issues that are important to them. Let's examine the strategy one more time.

Manager: *"Brad, thanks for coming in to meet with us today. Can you tell me a little about yourself?"*

Candidate: *"Well, since you have a snapshot of my work history already, I would add that I think I'm a good person, with a decent track record for success, but my guess is you may be looking for more than that to fill this* *position—perhaps some of the intangibles that don't show up as specific line items on a resume.*

For example, besides finding someone who is knowledgeable and experienced, you might be looking for someone who can ramp up in a short period of time to become productive as quickly as possible. You may want someone who can blend with the current culture, but also contribute new ideas and possibly a fresh perspective to the team. I'm guessing that you would also be looking for someone with a positive attitude, who is self-motivated and customer-focused.

If so, those are the types of things that have enabled me to be successful thus far, and that's what I would want to bring to this position as well."

If you look at this dialogue against the backdrop of what's most important to the customer, this interview has suddenly taken a very different tack than what normally happens when candidates just focus on their own qualifications. The hiring manager's first impression is likely to be, "Wow, this person really understands what is important to me, and he is clearly focused on what it takes to be a valuable asset to our company. What a refreshing change from all the other candidates who just drone on and on about themselves!"

What you really want is a competitive advantage. Somehow you want to separate yourself from other people who are being considered and you want customers to form a positive impression about the value you bring to the table. To accomplish this, you must be able to demonstrate that you have some understanding of what issues might be important to the decision maker, in this case, the hiring manager.

How can you know what issues *might* be important to the customer before you actually meet them? If you are indeed a serious candidate for the position, you would have researched the company on the Internet and you may have even 'Googled' the name of the hiring manager. Doing your homework in advance is fine, although you should be aware that other candidates would probably have visited the company's website as well. In addition to knowing some general information about the company, the key to really connecting with customers is to demonstrate an understanding of their specific issues.

The operative word here is 'demonstrate.' Don't worry, you don't have to dress in black, put on face paint, or crawl over the wall late at night to know what's important to prospective customers. All you really have to do is put yourself in their shoes for a couple minutes and think about what issues would likely be most important to you.

Just say to yourself, "What types of things would be important to me if I was the hiring manager?" You don't have to be clairvoyant to realize that attributes like knowledge, experience, ramp-up time, and productivity would all be desirable attributes for qualified candidates, and would probably be on the mind of most hiring managers. Likewise, you don't have to adjust your personality to talk intelligently about decision issues like blending with the current culture or bringing a fresh perspective to the team. These are some fundamental employee traits that would be pertinent to any job opportunity and appeal to virtually every hiring manager. The key to striking a chord of connection with decision makers is for candidates to proactively bring these relevant topics up to the customer, or the hiring manager, in order to differentiate yourself, spark their interest, and establish enough credibility to cause the conversation to subsequently take off. This is big!

Also, did you notice in the dialogue that four out of the first five sentences from the candidate were customer-focused, as opposed to self-serving? That's good because it conveys a perception that the hiring manager's requirements are more important than the candidate's personal agenda. You might as well be customer-focused, because I can assure you this is precisely how the hiring manager feels.

Companies aren't just hoping to give people good jobs, or further their career paths. They're trying to address certain business needs, and the job interview is their opportunity to evaluate whether or not you provide the best possible solution. The same principle applies to any sales situation—customers in a typical sales call don't consider buying just so you can make a sale. They're trying to address a need of some kind, and evaluate whether your product or service provides a valuable solution.

For the naysayers, it's true that making a good first impression doesn't replace the need for a solid performance during the rest of the decision process. If you completely bumbled the rest of the interview, as an example, any positive impressions that were initially formed would be quickly forgotten. Still, the credibility that can be earned by demonstrating that you do understand and care about the customer's needs gives you a tremendous opportunity to show off some of the intangible qualities that will hopefully differentiate you from other qualified candidates who have never even thought about what it means to be customer-focused. What's not to like?

Priming the Pump

It's a fair question to ask whether selling is more of a science or an art. Frankly, I believe that in order to become a consistent sales performer, you must master both parts. Looking at sales as a science creates consistency and repeatability. The art of selling, then, enables sales professionals to apply their repertoire of communication skills and specific techniques and adapt as appropriate given the situation.

The beauty of science is that it's predictable. The law of gravity, for example, never takes a day off, which enables us to presume that certain things will happen based on scientific fact.

Oddly enough, the natural laws of physics provide some of the best guidance for dealing with customers, particularly when forging new relationships with prospective buyers or trying to impress a potential employer. Since we know that people are often reluctant to share with someone they don't know or trust, let me suggest an idea that will enhance your ability to establish credibility, and gain even more traction when kicking off your needs development conversations. Let's call this technique *priming the pump*.

When I was fifteen years old, I was an active member of Troop 93—an enthusiastic group of Boy Scouts that met regularly at the American Legion Post just outside my hometown of Spencerport, New York. In addition to attending the weekly meetings, my brother and I also participated in several scout jamborees and summer camps, which gave us with an opportunity to get our hands dirty once in a while, and transform classroom learning into real-life experiences.

On one such outing, our scoutmaster led a small group on

a weekend road-trip down to the Southern Tier of New York state. There we camped with several other scout troops on a fifty acre wooded area situated next to a local farmer's corn field. That probably doesn't sound very glamorous, but it was still exciting to be out in the wilderness and on our own.

At some point on the trip, a fellow scout and I wandered into the deeper woods to see what trouble we could get into. A few hundred yards down the path, we happened upon a small ramshackle out-building, that upon further investigation, turned out to be a pump house for a fresh-water well. Have you ever seen one of those vintage cast iron pumps set into a concrete block with a large handle? As curious fifteen-year old boys, we felt an immediate urge to find out if the rusty old pump still worked. So, I grabbed the iron handle, and, using some muscle to get it started, strenuously pushed down to see if we could get water to come out. After a few mighty pumps, we got nothing. My friend and I mustered some extra energy and pumped even harder. Still, nothing came out. I bet we pumped that thing for twenty minutes before deciding that the well below the concrete base must be dry. Oh, well (yes, pun intended!).

When we got back to the campsite, we announced our discovery, and of course, the other boys all wanted to come see the pump house. "Wait," our scoutmaster said. "If you go back, you might try pouring a canteen full of water into the top of the pump and see if that does any good."

No one actually said it out loud, but I'm sure more than one of us was thinking, "Mr. Martin...duh! We're trying to get water to come out of the well, not pour water into it." He could tell by our faces we thought his idea was crazy, but he encouraged us to try it anyway. "What do adults know about pumping water?" we wondered as we wandered back into the forest.

Several boys took turns behind the large iron handle, pumping ferociously in an attempt to get water to come out. As before, the spigot on the end of the pump was bone dry. We pumped and pumped with no success. I don't recall who actually remembered Mr. Martin's sage advice, but one of the scouts had a canteen on his belt and offered it up as a last resort. It was worth trying since the strong-arm forceful approach was obviously not getting it done.

Carefully, we poured the canteen water into the top of the pump. I remember thinking, "This is the dumbest idea ever." Pouring water into the well was the exact opposite of what we were hoping to accomplish.

Then, came the moment of truth. I grabbed the giant pump handle and heaved downward with all the might a spindly fifteen year-old Boy Scout could muster. Nothing came out. Big surprise! So, I gathered my strength and pumped again. This time, the spigot end of the pump started to bubble and spit, and by the third pump, buckets of water started gushing out onto the surrounding concrete. I mean, water was splashing everywhere and most of us got soaked. We took turns drinking the fresh spring water and later reported back to camp where Mr. Martin basked in the glow of being right.

I didn't realize it at the time, but the most valuable lesson I learned that day didn't actually register with me until many years later when I was struggling to start a career in the sales profession. You see, when I first went into sales, I was taught the same way as everyone else—ask probative questions to uncover the prospect's needs. While calling on prospect accounts, I remember that the act of probing for needs felt like I was

pumping customers for information. Not surprisingly, the proverbial well of information was often dry. It quickly became apparent
to me that prospective customers were reluctant to share information with a salesperson they didn't yet know or trust, and the more
forcefully I pumped, the less information I got.

For decades, sellers have been taught to probe for needs by
asking open-ended questions like, "Mr. Customer, what are
your goals and objectives for the next five years?" A popular
alternative is, "What's the biggest issue that you currently face?"
Another perennial favorite is, "Ms. Customer, what keeps you
up at night?"

The truth is, most people don't want to be *pumped* for information. Customers will share their goals, issues, and concerns if
they perceive you to be a valuable resource, but no one wants to
be probed by an aggressive salesperson. We sure don't want to be
on the receiving end of rhetorical questions or something that
feels like an interrogation from an eager vendor rep.

If you have appropriately prepared yourself in advance
and you are willing to invest a few moments to *prime the
pump* of communication, the customer's reaction is likely to
be "gushingly" different. In the context of your next job interview, I already showed you how to prime the pump for more
in-depth conversation. You do this by proactively raising
issues that strike a chord with the hiring manager and convey
a perception that you are indeed a valuable, customer-focused
resource. Salespeople can just as easily prime the pump in
their needs development conversations by raising relevant
decision issues that actually contribute to the conversation
rather than expect customers to magically open up and share
all their needs with you.

In Chapters 4, 5, and 6, we will talk about needs development at length, in terms of *Conversational Dynamics, Decision Making 101*, and *How to be Strategic with Your Questions*, so let's not worry about building a script of specific questions just yet. However, I do want to show you how simple questions give sellers the ability to raise relevant business issues that might be important to the customers. For example:

Seller: *"How many service calls do you handle per day?"*
            "Do you send out customer satisfaction surveys?"
            "What percent of revenue comes from repeat business?"
            "Have you experienced a decrease in customer traffic given the recent economic slowdown?"

Besides gathering important data about the client, asking specific questions about business issues that *might* be important to the customer gives them the opportunity to form the impression that you are an intelligent, knowledgeable, customer-focused, valuable resource. These are just a few of the intangibles that will determine how successful you will be when selling yourself. In fact, by proactively raising relevant topics like *number of service calls per day, satisfaction surveys, revenue, customer traffic,* and *recent economic conditions,* you bolster your own credibility with prospective customers. From there, it's a simple matter of physics. A salesperson who contributes nothing of substance to their conversations probably won't get much substantive information in return. However, when you demonstrate the ability to raise and discuss issues that are indeed important to customers, don't be surprised when buckets of valuable information begin to flow in your direction. Therein lies the magic of taking a PAS approach—you bond with customers on their problems (P), not your solutions (S).

Tips for the Hiring Manager

If you are in a role that is responsible for making hiring decisions, here are five 'tells' that will help you determine whether a candidate would be a good hire. Applicants should pay attention, too, because understanding what hiring managers look for can provide useful insight as to how you conduct yourself in your next job interview or customer call.

i.) Was the candidate interested enough to ask questions, or did they simply respond to what was asked? If they were shy about asking, was it because they were intimidated, felt overwhelmed, or simply did not appear to be interested in the opportunity?

ii.) Did the candidate demonstrate they were prepared and had put some thought into the specific opportunity?

iii.) Was the candidate interested in your business and your specific hiring objectives? To what extent did they explore or raise important topics? Were they focused on helping you accomplish *your* goals?

iv.) How much of the candidate's pre-interview or follow up was done person-to-person as opposed to hiding behind the electronic veil of email or the Internet?

v.) What did the applicant do to differentiate themselves from other candidates interested in the position?

A good-looking, professional resume is definitely a plus if you seek a new career opportunity. But, any good salesperson will tell you that just having a nice 'product brochure' is not enough to guarantee your success in making the sale. The candidate must also demonstrate a certain confidence for how to conduct a meeting, and a vision for how they are going to be successful in the position.

Tips for Qualified Candidates

Beyond the numerous strategies and techniques already outlined in this book, here's one extra piece of advice I would offer with regard to the theme of selling yourself. Make sure you are prepared (in advance) to discuss your *vision* for how you *plan* to succeed in whatever you aspire to accomplish. Success rarely happens by accident, and if you were interviewing for a position within my company, the first thing I would want to know is, "Do you have a specific plan for being successful in this job?"

Successful people plan their work and they work their plans. They have a vision for what it takes to succeed and they also have an ability to communicate that vision to others. Since even

> "Successful people plan their work and they work their plans."

the best laid plans don't always pan out as we originally envision them, your ability to make reasonable adjustments along the way is also critically important to hiring managers. Shooting from the hip is no longer a viable strategy in today's business environment.

If I was interviewing you for a sales position, I would also want to understand your philosophy on selling. More importantly, I would want to know that you had a specific sales philosophy. Which sales courses have you attended and what books have you read? Of all the candidates being considered, why should I hire you?

Make it your mission to be one who stands out, even to the point of creating a strategy binder and bringing a specific business plan to the job interview. Present it like you were already in charge of the division. It's perfectly acceptable to make assumptions that allow for flexibility during the implementation phases of your plan. You can even make ongoing revisions as you acclimate to the position an integral part of your plan.

Potential employers are just like prospective customers in the sense that they want to know that you are confident in your abilities, and you have the foresight and fortitude necessary to make things happen in ways that will benefit them and you.

Even with a notable track record, we must recognize that in a competitive environment, you will rarely be the only candidate (or vendor) being considered. Other qualified candidates will also garner a serious look. Hence, the purpose of an employment interview is not just to review one's honors and accolades from the past. The real purpose of these evaluations is to give the hiring manager or a prospective customers a glimpse into the future so they can evaluate which alternative provides the best fit in helping them achieve their goals.

In the final analysis, *you* must make the difference. To the extent you are able to demonstrate that your skills are aligned with the customer's goals, you can expect a great deal of success going forward. On the other hand, if you sound just like everyone else, then you put your destiny in the hands of a virtual coin flip at best. It's that simple. *Selling yourself* during an interview or with regard to a product sale has everything to do with the customer's perception of *you*.

Chapter 4

Managing
Conversational Dynamics™

What if it was possible to remove the pressure and awkwardness we sellers often feel when probing for needs, dealing with price objections, or when you're trying to close a sale?

Reducing conversational tension is where superior sales technique gives the strategic salesperson a significant advantage. As you have probably heard many times, it's not just what you say (or ask) that's important, your success is also contingent how those messages (or questions) are actually being delivered.

Have you ever wondered why some conversations with customers seem to flow along with inexplicable ease, while other times it feels like you're pulling teeth to initiate a dialogue or suggest possible next steps? Consistent with the overall theme of this book, the extent to which other people are open to answering your questions, listening to your ideas, or receptive to hearing your advice is largely a reflection of how you choose to communicate with them.

Most QBS clients are hungry for any ideas, suggestions, or

strategies that will give them a competitive edge. But, there's no point in running around telling salespeople what they already know—like that it's important to uncover the customer's needs, propose valuable solutions, or close sales. Everyone already knows the obvious basics. What sellers really want is insight and guidance for *how* to effectively execute on these sales goals. More specifically, they want to understand *how* to penetrate new opportunities, especially given a changing business climate. They also want to know *how* to create a differentiable advantage in a marketplace where competitors all claim to offer the best solutions, and *how* to secure more mindshare with key decision makers in important target accounts. *How* can you motivate customers who are 'on the fence,' and increase their sense of urgency to move forward with a decision? Also, what's the best way to wrap up the sales transaction without having to stress the very relationships you've worked so hard to build?

In sales, achieving trusted advisor status seems to be the Holy Grail in terms of placing yourself in the strongest possible position to close deals. Why? Because customers usually do business with the person from whom they feel most comfortable taking advice. You have to assume that some vendor is going to have the decision maker's ear. The challenge in today's competitive marketplace is positioning yourself to be the one who ends up in the coveted 'trusted advisor' role.

To become an effective advice-giver, however, whoever is on the receiving end of your insight must be open and willing to listen to, consider, and heed your recommendations. Salespeople, managers, and sales trainers all agree that education plays a significant role in the decision making process. Having the ability to clearly communicate the value of your solution is a valuable sales skill. But, effective communication is a two-way street. In addition to positioning the value of your product or service, your probability of success is also contingent on the receptiveness of your audience. Consequently, it's no longer enough for sellers to convey a strong message. You must also be able to cause customers to "want to" hear it.

That raises an interesting question. If the receptivity of your audience greatly contributes to your success, perhaps we should ask, is there anything a salesperson can do to influence a customer's receptivity?

I must tell you that I'm not a fan of manipulative sales tactics, nor do I believe that your sales approach should be built around the idea of trying to control other people. Decision makers are going to form impressions, interpret your product's value proposition, and reach conclusions on their own, whether we like it or not. In fact, trying to force your own agenda on other people generally takes a salesperson into dangerous territory, since most customers are only going to act on something if they perceive it best suits their objectives. How do you *force* prospective customers to become interested in your product or service anyway? Moreover, how do you force someone to recommend your proposal to their colleagues or boss? It becomes easy for me to conclude that subversive attempts to manipulate or overpower a customer's own judgment can actually do more to hurt your sales efforts than help.

While trying to "control" other people is indeed a flawed strategy, sellers fortunately do have the opportunity to control our own actions, especially if we recognize that how we choose to deal with prospects and customers can directly influence the perceptions they form about us. And, just as a salesperson can harm or damage a relationship by doing something silly or out of context, you can also help yourself significantly by paying attention to the dynamics of your sales conversations.

Conversational dynamics refers to the intangible subtleties that affect the natural flow of your sales conversations, and the rest of your interpersonal interactions for that matter. Understanding how the subtleties of your interactions influence the perceptions other people form about you enables sellers to facilitate more productive conversations. If the real purpose of a job interview is get a feel for which candidate provides the best fit, the purpose of a sales conversation is for customers to form impressions about the potential value of a proposed solution, coupled with their impression of the value provided by the person representing that product or service.

Given that *how* you choose to represent yourself influences the perceptions other people form about your company and your solutions, one of the easiest ways to increase your value in the eyes of your target market is to proactively manage the dynamics of your sales conversations.

The object of this chapter is not psychological—just logical. Personally, I'm averse to manipulative sales tactics because most people (including myself) don't want to be manipulated by a salesperson. Fortunately for us, causing potential customers to "want to" engage in productive conversation about their decision objectives and your corresponding solutions has nothing to do with manipulative tactics. Instead, it's about building mutually beneficial business relationships.

It's been said many times that selling would be a lot more fun if it were somehow possible to eliminate the risk of rejection and fear of failure that often accompany critical milestones in the sales process. In fact, Question Based Selling was originally developed as a risk reduction strategy, recognizing that a salesperson's success is directly related to helping customers accomplish their goals. It just so happens that reducing a salesperson's risk of failure is also the single most effective way to increase your probability of success. The good news is, communicating effectively doesn't have to feel awkward or be difficult if you are willing to pay attention to how you are being perceived.

Securing the Customer's Permission

Much of the awkwardness sellers feel when engaging potential customers occurs during the opening exchange, and then again at various points of transition throughout the conversation. Particularly if you deal with prospects who hold salespeople off at arm's length, it's important to get the timing right if you want to easily transition from the introductory stage of your sales conversations into needs development, or from needs development into the product presentation phase. Most of the tension comes from the inherent risk of rejection sellers face, knowing that cautious customers are aren't always willing to yield to our desired path in the conversation. If you can just get the dialogue rolling, both parties in the conversation often relax to the point where buyers and sellers can focus on the issues at hand.

One of the keys to being effective in sales is the ability to gain traction (credibility and perceived value) early in the dialogue, in order to then transition through the rest of the conversation with relative ease. Mind you, most customers are pretty smart and they understand that to get valuable advice from vendors, they must be willing to provide some relevant information about their needs. When you go to a doctor, for example, you must first provide some specific information about the status of your health, in order for the doctor to prescribe an appropriate remedy or recommendation. The same principle applies when you meet with an accountant or attorney.

> "Customers must be willing to share information if they want a salesperson to provide valuable advice or potential solutions."

You want these professionals to understand your specific needs before rendering an opinion or recommending solutions.

The sales profession is no different in this regard. At some point, customers must be willing to share some pertinent information if they want a salesperson to provide valuable advice or recommend potential solutions. The catch is, decision makers simply aren't willing to engage with every vendor who happens to come calling. This creates a bit of a paradox, where customers want new ideas and valuable solutions, but they are reticent to sharing information with someone they don't yet know or trust.

What if it were possible to sidestep the standoffishness sellers often encounter from customers, and instead, cause potential buyers to be more inviting and also more receptive to engaging us in more productive conversations? In fact, wouldn't it be great if sellers could push a magic button that would cause the customer to say something like, "Sure, Mr. Salesperson, go ahead and ask me questions so we can have a valuable exchange of information." Or, suppose you could get a potential buyer to say, "Ms. Salesperson, can you help me better understand the value of your products?" Either of these requests from a customer would provide a wonderful entrée for you to facilitate a needs development conversation, or educate them on the value of your solutions.

I'll let you in on one of the most important and valuable secrets from *Question Based Selling*. If someone actually *invites* you to ask them questions, when you do ask, you get exponentially more information (in response) than if you had simply bulled ahead with your own agenda. Similarly, when someone *invites* you to educate them on your solutions, or actually asks for your opinion, you will get significantly more mindshare and time in front of that person to present your ideas. It's only logical that someone who invites you to "engage" is going to be more open to sharing information and receiving advice.

Ah, back to reality—unfortunately, there is no magic button that sellers can push. I do have an idea for you, however, that can produce the same result. It's a technique called *manufacturing a mini-invitation*, which is almost magical in terms of engaging potential customers in more productive conversations.

Leveraging Mini-Invitations

If you study human interaction, you will notice that it's difficult to initiate a dialogue, or take the conversation deeper, without some spark of "invitation" from the other person enabling you to get into more depth. More simply stated, it's easier to advance a conversation if the person you are talking with invites you to proceed, as opposed to just charging ahead. But, rather than sitting back and hoping that customers will issue an unsolicited carte blanche invitation, sellers can actually manufacture these *mini-invitations* by using proven question-based techniques.

Back when I officially left the corporate world to develop Question Based Selling, one of the questions that people used to ask me is, "What made you decide to stop selling?"

It turns out that I am still very much in sales. Only now, I'm responsible for selling myself and my company. What a novel concept! My company, QBS Research, Inc. offers a full slate of sales development products and services, everything from QBS Methodology Training, QBS OnLine, QBS books and QBS audio programs, in addition to the various speaking engagements I deliver. Accordingly, I spend a great deal of time talking with sales managers and executives about their goals and objectives and how our company might be able to provide value.

Sometimes, potential clients jump right in and ask, "How much does a QBS training class cost?" I don't mind if someone asks me about price. To me, that sounds like an invitation. If you think about it, the client is really saying, "Tom, can you help me understand the value of your offering, relative to how much it costs, so I can make an informed decision?" If you represent a viable product, you want prospective clients to invite you to share details that will help them make informed decisions.

Thirty minutes later, another potential client might say, "Can you tell me about Question Based Selling?" Sounds a little like a job interview, doesn't it? Like when a hiring manager says, "Tom, tell me about yourself."

Whether the client asks about cost or they want an overview of our training programs, my response is basically the same.

Freese: *"I'm happy to provide you with all the details about the different QBS programs and how much they cost. Can I ask you a couple specifics about your sales*

> *organization in order to give you relevant, accurate information?"*

VP of Sales: *"Sure, go ahead."*

It's very predictable that their answer is going to be, "Yes." I mean, who wouldn't want relevant and accurate information? In this simple example, the *dynamics* of the conversation have shifted dramatically, from the customer's original request which would have sent me down the path of focusing on price, to the customer actually inviting me to ask them a series of specific questions to better understand their needs. The net effect is that my choice of words creates a significantly more receptive audience. As a result, the conversation has instantly shifted to a path that will end up being most beneficial to the customer—understanding their needs.

I simply *manufactured a mini-invitation*. Because of the way I responded to the client's inquiry, they could either grant me permission to ask a "couple specifics," or not. I tell clients to expect a 99.9% probability that customers will say, "Yes...," "Sure...," "Go ahead," "No problem," or, "Absolutely!" If your customer would have answered any question you could have asked, they will respond affirmatively to this one.

Why are potential customers so willing to grant their permission? It's because of the way my question was framed. By inviting me to "ask a couple specifics about...," I have now positioned the conversation in a way that the customer is essentially accomplishing their own objective of getting relevant and accurate information. That's what most customers really want anyway—a salesperson who is forthright and willing to provide details, yet customer-focused enough to realize that some specific information is needed in order to provide valuable recommendations.

Customers who would otherwise be reserved and stand-offish toward salespeople will suddenly open up and share tons of information once they have invited you to ask. This simple technique of manufacturing mini-invitations causes an instantaneous reduction in a client's natural defense mechanisms. Because the other person is essentially giving me permission to ask questions, I am virtually guaranteed to receive a more valuable response.

> "Manufacturing mini-invitations causes an instantaneous reduction in a client's natural defense mechanisms."

Like many of the softer skills in selling, the significance of this mini-invitation strategy can easily be lost in its subtlety. By securing a customer's permission to ask questions, the dynamics of the conversation instantly shifts out of 'spew mode' and into discovery. This is not a strategy for dodging the customer's request. On the contrary, I'm happy to tell potential clients about our programs and how much they cost. But, like most things, recommending the best alternative requires that I know a few basic facts about the nature of the request, like: Is the client more interested in QBS methodology training or a speaking engagement? Where will their event be held? How many people are expected to attend? Are they targeting specific dates?

Notice that the client's invitation materializes as the result of good communication technique. This is important because it puts you in control of your own destiny to foster more productive conversations, and also, to repeat your success. The logic behind conversational dynamics is simple—by asking permission and being respectful of the other person's right not to share with you, you essentially lower the customer's defenses in a way that assures you will get much more information. Who knew that being respectful and responsive to customers could also be extremely productive?

Perfecting the Technique

Perhaps the best and most frequent example of where this strategy of manufacturing mini-invitations can be helpful is to seamlessly transition your sales conversations into needs development. If fact, there is only one time in Question Based Selling where I recommend exact words. At the appropriate time in the dialogue, you simply say, *"Mr. Smith, can I ask you a couple specifics about _____."*

Let's go back to the interview analogy from Chapters 2 and 3, and see what happens when we apply this idea of manufacturing a mini-invitation to the first part of the job interview.

Manager: *"Tom, thanks for coming in to meet with us today. Can you tell me a little about yourself?"*

Candidate: *"Well, since you already have my resume, I would add that I am a hard working person with a decent track record. But, my guess is you may be looking for more than that to fill this position—perhaps some of the intangibles that don't always show up on a resume. For example, besides finding someone with knowledge and experience, I'm guessing that you* *would want someone who could ramp up and become productive as soon as possible. You might also be looking for someone who can blend well with the current culture, as well as contribute a fresh perspective to the team. As long as we're hypothesizing, you may also be looking for someone with a positive attitude, who is self-motivated and extremely customer-focused. Am I close?"*

Manager: *"You're right on the money."*

Candidate: *"Well, can I ask you a couple specifics about the job so I can get a better sense of the opportunity?"*

Manager: *"Sure, go right ahead."*

Selling yourself in today's competitive marketplace requires more than just answering whatever questions you happen to get asked. You must also be able to manage the dynamics of your conversations to keep the dialogue on track and make the best of your time with customers. Don't worry, the interviewer (or customer) won't even realize that you are using QBS techniques. Hiring managers want qualified candidates to show interest in the position being offered, and there's no better way to demonstrate your interest than asking "a couple specifics" about the opportunity.

This strategy of manufacturing mini-invitations is not limited to the beginning of a sales conversation, however. Mini-invitations can also be valuable conversational tools to transition a dialogue from needs development into your product presentation, or to suggest possible next steps.

For example, once you've exhausted the needs development

portion of your conversation, and it's time to educate the customer on your potential solutions, you can easily use this same technique to further manufacture additional mini-invitations. You simply say,

Seller: *"Mr. Customer, thanks for giving me an overview of your organization and your current business environment. Would it be valuable for me to explain the different solution alternatives we offer and how they might impact your organization?"*

Just like before, if the customer is interested in hearing about your offerings, they will intuitively say, "Sure, go ahead." Bingo!

Using Mini-Invitations in Everyday Life

Even though I had been using mini-invitations in my business dealings for a long time, I didn't really start thinking about why this technique was so valuable until I started using it in my everyday life. So, whether you are socializing at a neighborhood dinner party, chaperoning a teenage youth group, or serving on a charitable committee at your kids' school or church, you will discover countless opportunities in your daily routine where this very same technique works to perfection.

Part of my epiphany came as the result of my serving on various church committees over the years. I used to find these experiences frustrating and enlightening at the same time. You see, my style in business is to net-out a situation, understand the options for moving forward, and then make a decision. Thus, I have a tendency to share ideas with people as they pop into my head, rather than being patient (or strategic) and waiting for just the right moment. I don't say everything that pops into my brain, but when I think of something really good, I tend to get excited and want to share it—right now!

The trouble is, particularly when you are dealing with a team of volunteers, like on a church committee, it's an understatement to say that not everyone moves at the same pace. So, after enough of my best ideas fell on deaf ears, it started to occur to me that just blurting out my thoughts on a particular subject wasn't working. The truth is, if Delores was still pondering the color of the napkins needed for the churchwide picnic, then let's not be surprised if she wasn't exactly ready to be receptive to another suggestion regarding some other topic.

I wish this revelation about using mini-invitations had come sooner because it would have saved me a lot of time and headaches. Once I realized people were not going to change their nature, I decided to adjust my own approach to see if that would make people more receptive. Now, whenever I want to share an idea at a church meeting or neighborhood dinner party, I am much more inclined to say, "You know, I just thought of something that could save us a bunch of time and money."

Invariably, someone in the gathering will respond by saying, "What's your idea?" Then, I share. If you give people a chance to acknowledge that they are indeed interested in what you have to say, they are much more likely to be receptive to your ideas, and thus, more likely to actually consider the information or advice being offered.

This same technique works just as well when dealing with teenagers. My fourth book is actually a "sales" book called, *The Question Based Parent*. From experience, it's clear to me that kids (just like adults) need to buy into your vision if you want your ideas or guidance to have an actual impact on them. In that vein, we are always selling. Ever noticed how young people aren't always eager to be on the receiving end of advice from adults, especially their parents? Next time you want to offer a budding teen some advice, try manufacturing a mini-invitation first. Say, "Can I make a suggestion that might spare you some grief next time this happens?" You may have to give them a minute to exhale dramatically and roll their eyes, but if you can be patient, your teen will ultimately say (or grunt) something that essentially means, "Sure, go ahead."

In my first book, I wrote, "Spending a few minutes to make someone feel special is more important than spending hours to make them feel average." People who feel respected are quick to invite you to ask questions and are much more open to hearing your advice.

Understanding Question-Based Logic

People are often surprised when they learn that Question Based Selling isn't just about teaching people how to ask questions. Frankly, it's a shame that traditional sales trainers have placed so much emphasis on the desire to gather information, uncover needs, and qualify opportunities, without regard to the fact that customers are generally reluctant to share with a salesperson they don't yet know or trust. Call me crazy, but I would argue that if someone doesn't *want to* share with you, then it doesn't matter what you ask—the conversation will end right there. Hence, the real skill with regard to selling yourself is causing customers to want to open up and share valuable information with *you*.

We sellers totally have an agenda. We want to understand the customer's needs in order to provide valuable solutions. It's okay to have goals. After all, identifying opportunities is ultimately what drives every company's bottom line. But, customers have agendas, too. They're dealing with problems, issues, and goals, in addition to wanting to satisfy certain wants and desires. Only if a product or service seems to provide a good fit might they be willing to listen, and then only to the extent that the salesperson makes a valuable use of their time. This is where question-based logic comes in—logic, not just questions.

Personally, I like the idea of securing the customer's permission prior to asking questions. Do you think customers today would rather deal with someone who is polite and respectful or would they rather sellers just plow ahead with their own self-serving agendas? Knowing that a mini-invitation from the customer instantly paves the way to more productive conversation, it is very easy for me to think in terms of saying, "Ms. Customer. I'd be happy to give you all the details. Can I ask you a couple specifics about your upcoming project?"

Asked at the appropriate time, customers will surely say, "Yes." This is not about fooling people into answering questions a certain way. It's about being customer-focused, respectful, and demonstrating that you want to make the best use of the decision maker's time. In fact, the word "specifics" is usually music to the customer's ears, because they either want to get specific or they would rather not be dealing with you at all. Customers are tired of marketing hype and they're even less excited about sitting though another generic sales pitch.

Getting Your Foot in the Door

Mini-invitations are particularly valuable early in the sales process when you're trying to break into a competitive marketplace like the insurance business, real estate, or selling manufactured goods. In these highly competitive businesses, one vendor's value proposition is often very similar to the rest, to the point where customers who are already satisfied with their current supplier may not even bother entertaining discussions with other vendors. In those cases, sellers must find some way to pique the customer's interest and lower their defenses—at the same time.

My friend Bart Burton and his brother, Bill, started a business in Little Rock, Arkansas, selling print supplies. Since we are well into the electronic age, Bart assumed that most of his target customers probably had a supplier already, from whom they purchased print supplies and toner cartridges. Penetrating new accounts was sure be a challenge, especially if they sounded just like every other cold-caller who walked through the customer's door.

Now, whenever the Burton brothers get in front of a potential buyer, their strategy focuses on piquing the office manager's interest and creating a mini-invitation that will then pave the way into a more in-depth conversation. Check it out.

Salesperson: *"Hi, Ms. Jones, my name is Bart Burton with Integrated Printing Supplies here in Little Rock. I realize that you may have a source for office equipment already, which is perfectly fine. We specialize in print supplies. But, the value we offer to customers is* *unique because we basically solve the problems that traditional toner vendors have created, and we save customers money in the process."*

Office Mgr: *"What problems do you solve?"*

What the customer is really saying here is, "Can you give me more information so I can know how you might be able to help us?" Doesn't that sound like a nice invitation from an otherwise standoffish prospect? If the office manager is at all curious about what problems Bart is referring to, she will absolutely invite him to educate her on his value proposition. Perfect! What happens next is pretty straight forward, especially if you implement the strategy from Chapter 3, remembering that your greatest opportunity to provide value starts with a discussion about the customer's problems, issues, and concerns (P).

Salesperson: *"Well, there are a lot of tricks that get pulled by vendors in the toner business. Things like overstocking the customer's supply shelves, substituting lesser quality products, or not keeping enough inventory and allowing customers to run out of product at the least opportune time. We are able to eliminate these issues because of how our service is set up. Would it make sense for me to give you a quick overview of how we do it?"*

The phrase, "Would it make sense to…," is particularly effective from a *conversational dynamics* perspective. Instead of being driven by the hope of making a sales commission, you are now bringing logic and sensibility into play. If you are recommending an appropriate next step, it probably does "make sense" for the customer to have more information about your solution, which creates yet another invitation. By the way, the reason your suggested next step does 'make sense' is because it gives customers the insight they need to make a decision that ultimately addresses their requirements.

A telesales person could just as easily say, "Would it make sense for us to schedule one of our representatives to come out and show you how our solutions would impact your business?"

This same technique also works as a trial close. At the appropriate time in the sales process, you can say, "Mr. Customer, would it make sense for us to move forward with a smaller quantity in order to prove the product?"

"How familiar are you with...?"

Sellers can use a variation on this technique to manufacture additional mini-invitations when kicking-off a product presentation. Basically, you take the guesswork and any awkwardness out of where to begin. Otherwise, should you assume the customer knows nothing about your product and risk offending knowledgeable buyers, or would it be better to presume some level of knowledge already, and let customers stop you if they get confused? Since clairvoyance is not one of my strengths, I would rather just ask, *"Mr. Customer, how familiar are you with the different type of training programs we offer?"*

If the customer says, "I've been to your website but that's about all," their response tells me exactly where to begin my presentation—at the beginning. The next prospect may say, "I attended one of your courses a couple months ago, so I'm pretty familiar with your training." For them, I would start my presentation in a much different place. Either way, the customer's response lets me know where to start, as they are essentially saying, "Go ahead and present your solutions…but please begin here." By knowing upfront how familiar the customer is with our solutions, my job as a salesperson instantly becomes much easier.

The way you deliver the question is important, too. For example, don't ask, "*Are* you familiar with…?" Sounds similar, doesn't it? It's not. Asking someone if they "are familiar" with something tends to generate a yes/no response, which not only doesn't provide much feedback, prospects will often say "Yes" just because they don't want to seem ignorant or uninformed. Also, if your customer says, "Yes, I am familiar with your products," your opportunity to educate them shrinks significantly—because of your words. Instead, make it a point to ask, "*How* familiar are you with…?" This will cause them to quantify their answer. Here's an example.

Seller:	*"I would be happy to review the different options with you. Can I ask you a couple specifics about the project in order to give you more accurate information?"*
Buyer:	*"Sure, go ahead."*
Seller:	*"How familiar are you with the various secondary insurance coverages that are now being offered to seniors?"*

Even if a potential buyer claims to be the absolute expert on your product, you can easily say, "Well, there have been a couple updates and new announcements in recent weeks. Would it be valuable for me to bring you up to speed?" Instantly they wonder, *what recent updates?* Exactly!

A Certain Precision is Required

In addition to having trained thousands of salespeople over the years, I have also coached my fair share of sales managers. That said, here's a quick coaching tip with regard to selling yourself. *Almost* doing it right isn't always close enough in today's competitive marketplace. You need a certain amount of precision to execute consistently.

For example, oftentimes when I deliver an Advanced QBS Training as a follow up, it's not at all unusual for someone in the audience to say, "Tom, I tried one of your techniques but it didn't work."

> "*Almost* doing it right isn't always close enough in today's competitive marketplace. You must be precise to execute consistently."

"Really, what happened?" I ask.

They proceed to tell me that they said to the customer, "I would like to ask you a few questions about..."

Can you spot the problem? A tiny change in wording can end up making a HUGE difference in results. It is possible that this particular salesperson encountered a rogue customer who was in a foul mood one day. Granted, there are going to be some situations where nothing works. But, it's usually pretty easy to identify the culprit when something's not right.

In this case, let's start with punctuation. *I would like to ask you a few questions about…* is not a question. As the founder of Question Based Selling, I teach people to be question-based, not statement-based. Whenever a salesperson announces, "I would like to (do anything)," let's not be surprised if that sounds self-serving to the customer. In fact, almost any sentence that begins with, "I would like to…," tends to automatically increase a customer's natural defense mechanisms, making them even more standoffish. Oops!

"But, Tom, what I said was close to what you suggested," they sometimes assert. Again, there is only one time in all of Question Based Selling where I recommend exact words. At the appropriate time in the conversation, usually when you are in a suitable position to kick off the needs development conversation, you simply say, *"Mr. Customer, can I ask you a couple specifics about _____?"* Their response will undoubtedly be, "Yes." If you recognize that a certain amount of precision is required to be successful at anything, it's just not that hard to execute this phrase exactly as planned.

Sometimes, even the most loyal advocates of QBS will comment about certain techniques, saying, "It feels different," or, "That's just not my style." Since I'm not a believer in verbatim sales scripts, I have no problem when a salesperson uses their own judgment to decide where specific question-based techniques apply or don't. But, for the record, let me say that the need to adapt everything to your own personal style is overrated. If something in this book seems logical, or at least makes enough sense to try it, if it ends up being successful over and over again, I can assure you that it will very quickly become part of your style. Granted, you may have to step outside your comfort zone in order to try something the first time. But, I can tell you that these techniques and strategies have been time tested in many different cultures, and proven thousands of times over, so there's no need to reinvent the wheel.

Don't Treat Price as an Objection

In pretty much every type of selling, price is the number one objection. Most sellers know it's going to come up at some point. Not only do customers need to cost-justify the purchase, some buyers will try to beat you up on price simply because it's part of the sport of negotiation.

Sellers often dread these conversations about price. I don't, because asking about the cost of a product or service is a legitimate request and an important element in any decision. Later in the book, I dedicate an entire chapter to *Selling Intangibles & Cost Justification*. The problem comes when decision makers focus on price so early that your offerings get commoditized and the advantages your solution offers go unnoticed. That's why sellers usually cringe when the very first question out of a prospect's mouth is, "How much does it cost?"

In terms of conversational dynamics, when customers ask about price, they're usually not just trying to find out how much something costs. You might wonder, "How can you say that, Tom? I get asked about price all the time!" I'm aware that sellers are getting 'beaten up' on the issue of price. I, myself, encounter a steady stream of clients every week asking me to help them deal with the price issue. Fortunately, I can show you a very effective way to sidestep the traditional risks associated with these early price requests.

You would probably be very happy to talk with potential

customers about the price of your product or service, just not as the very first topic of conversation. So, rather than dreading whether or not the question of cost will come up, what if it was possible to completely reframe the customer's request in a way that sparks a more in-depth conversation about their needs and your corresponding value? Watch. Wouldn't it be cool if a customer asked the following:

Customer: *"Mr. Seller, can you please help me understand the cost of your product and how it compares with other alternatives so I can make a wise decision?"*

If you could get a customer to actually say these words, wouldn't that be music to a salesperson's ears? Besides being a polite and reasonable request, the customer would clearly be asking for the salesperson's help, which is good because the subsequent pricing discussion should revolve around how your proposed solutions match up to their needs. Since customers will ultimately base their purchase decision on your product's cost effectiveness, helping customers understand how your product or service compares to other options is what most decision makers really want when they ask about price, anyway.

So, let me show you how it all flows together.

Buyer: *"How much will this cost?"*

—the real request is —
"Can you help me understand the cost of your product and how it compares with other alternatives so I can make an informed decision?"

Seller: *"Sure, I'd be happy to give you all the details about our programs and their related costs. Can I ask you a couple specifics about your project in order to provide you with accurate information?"*

Buyer: *"Sure, go ahead."*

While I am eager and willing to share cost with qualified customers, it's important to shift the focus of the conversation long enough to understand what the customer actually needs. Once I understand what someone is really trying to accomplish, then I can educate them on whichever options would be most cost-effective to satisfy their objectives.

Deflection is a Strategic No-No

While it is reasonable for sellers to understand a customer's objectives before just spewing out prices, you must avoid the trap of sounding like you are dodging the customer's question. Here's a classic example of what *not* to say.

Customer: *"How much would you charge to implement the entire system?"*

Salesman: *"Before I tell you the price, I would first like to ask you a few questions."*

This salesperson might have noble intentions, and perhaps they even recognize the importance of understanding a customer's needs before diving into a price discussion. The problem is in the words he uses and the perception it creates.

Honestly, most customers are not really interested in changing the direction of the conversation just because a salesperson "would like" to ask some questions first.

If we examine more closely what just occurred, we see that when a customer asks about cost, the salesperson responds by saying, "Instead of talking about what you would like to discuss, Mr. Customer, I'm going to take you down a different path in the conversation." This is a classic example of deflection, and most customers won't stand for it. While he may think he's trying to help the customer by not just tossing out random prices, the customer is more likely to think, "I asked about cost. Why can't you just give me a price?"

Techniques Become the Differentiator

I'm not encouraging you to engage in an emotional battle of wits with potential customers. Furthermore, there's no guarantee you will win a sale because of a few neatly worded sentences. The goal when leveraging mini-invitations is simply to pave the way to more productive conversations with potential customers about their needs, and to provide them with enough information for them to make sound decisions.

After I changed my own approach as a territory salesperson, I suddenly started blowing out my sales numbers year after year. People who went on sales calls with me would say afterwards, "There's nothing magical about Tom Freese." That's true. I'm a regular person, just like you. "But," they would add, "it's amazing how eager customers are to share account details and other information with him." That was true, as well.

My DNA was no better than my competitors'. In many

cases, I was competing against vendors whose products were just as solid as mine. My advantage was really in my approach to dealing with customers. I believe that customers are going to be sharing their thoughts, feelings, and concerns with somebody, I just wanted to make sure it was me. Of course, once I figured out how to cause decision makers to share tons of information with me, while they naturally held my competitors off at arm's length, life was good.

Back then, no one had ever heard of a mini-invitation, and sellers were much more focused on *telling* than selling. Frankly, lots of salespeople are still in that mindset today. However, you now have the opportunity to adjust your approach, and more importantly, change the way you are being perceived in the marketplace. But, don't delay. If your customers are not "inviting" you to ask them questions, or inviting you to educate them on your offerings, then chances are good they are inviting one of your competitors to help them—perhaps someone like me.

Chapter 5

Influencing the Customer's Buying Criteria

I bet your local hardware store sells drills and drill bits. But, very few customers actually want the drill itself. What they really want are holes. Isn't that odd? Hardware stores don't sell what the customer really wants—holes. Purchasing a drill, therefore, simply becomes the means necessary to accomplish the desired result.

In the same manner, the decision to purchase your product or service usually is a way to accomplish some other objective or goal. Knowing the customer's true motivations, therefore, is very important. And, giving customers multiple reasons to buy from you can boost your sales while significantly benefiting the customer.

Customers buy products for a variety of reasons. That's actually a good thing, since the needs of individual decision makers can span a wide range of different priorities and hot buttons, not to mention the fact that personal preference, personality, and previous buying experiences also impact a customer's decisions making tendencies. One thing is certain, however. At some point in the sales process, something will either motivate potential buyers to move forward with a decision to purchase, or cause them to decline.

Why do you suppose some buyers are comfortable and ready to purchase, while other decision makers hesitate or inexplicably turn away from what seems to be a worthy transaction? It's because the decision to move forward with a purchase ultimately comes down to the customer's perception of your value proposition—specifically, whether the value of your proposed solution is great enough to justify the expenditure.

There's that word again—*value*. One of the things that makes selling a challenge is the realization that the actual value of your product or service is less important than how it is being perceived by prospective customers. In fact, I would submit that there is no such thing as *actual value*. While your product or service might seem extremely valuable to one prospect, that doesn't necessarily mean it will be perceived the same way by the next. Like they say about physical beauty, the perception of your value is in the eye of the beholder.

> "The actual value of your product or service is less important than how it is being perceived by prospective customers."

Let me try to put this in perspective using a parable that demonstrates the difference between what happens when customers perceive lots of value versus when they don't. I often demonstrate this to audiences when delivering live QBS training events.

When we come to the topic of perceived value, I reach down inside my computer bag and pull out a crisp $100 bill. Everyone's eyes instantly light up. Usually, I ask someone in the front row to verify that I am holding a bona fide $100 bill, and not play money or some slight-of-hand prop. Then, I pick out someone else in the audience and ask them, "Would you be willing to give me $20 in exchange for this $100 bill that I'm holding in my hand?"

There's no trick. You're either willing to trade your $20 for my $100, or you aren't. Most people jump at the idea, reaching for their wallet or purse as if I was offering a winning lottery ticket. Why wouldn't you want to take advantage of such a lucrative deal? Of course, everyone gets a quick chuckle when I qualify this offer as being only "hypothetical."

The point is, it's an easy decision. Agreeing to move forward with my proposed trade would net the lucky person a quick 5x return on their investment.

With that image fresh in everyone's mind, I reach down and put the $100 bill back into my computer bag. In the same motion, I stand back up with my hands cupped together to conceal what's inside. Then, holding my hands out to the audience, I say, "Ladies and Gentlemen, I am holding something in my hands. This is not a gag. I am definitely holding something, and it's something you would like *very* much if you got it."

People sometimes guess that my cupped hands are filled with air, thinking there must be a catch, and air *is* valuable. But, I quickly let the audience know that I definitely holding an item of some sort.

I ask the audience, "Who would be willing to give me $20 in exchange for the concealed item that I am now holding in my hands?" Strangely, no one is reaching for their wallet this time. I even walk up to individuals and directly ask them, "Do you have $20 in your wallet?" Most people do. "Can I see it?" Out comes their $20 to show me that they're not broke. "Would you be willing to trade your $20 for the item I am holding (still concealed) in my hands?"

"No, thanks," is always the answer.

"How about you, sir? Do you have $20?" I ask, turning to the unsuspecting person in the next seat.

"Can you tell me more about the item in your hands?" they sometimes ask.

"Sure," I say with a big smile. "It is a valuable item that you will definitely like a lot. In fact, I guarantee it!"

Sometimes they pause for a moment, but still the answer is, "No." One person after another politely declines my offer as I wander around the room with cupped hands.

Once it's clear that no one is willing to pay $20 for whatever I am holding in my hands, I reveal the item. It's the same crisp $100 bill that I held up earlier. Imagine that! I was offering to trade $100 for $20, only no one in the room was willing to take the risk.

What's the lesson in all of this? In the first scenario, where I was offering my $100 in trade for a significantly lesser amount, people could see the value of the deal. And, when it was perfectly clear that I was offering a good deal, they were more than willing to make a decision on the spot. They didn't have to check with their spouse, or put it into the budget for the following year. When the proposed value of a product or service clearly exceeds the cost to procure it, it's easy for people to pull the trigger and make a buying decision.

> "When the proposed value of a product or service clearly exceeds the cost to procure it, it's easy for people to pull the trigger and make a buying decision."

On the other hand, when the value of the deal being offered is ambiguous or unclear, as with the item concealed in my hands, decision makers tend to hesitate and retreat rather than moving forward. With the exception of a few riverboat gambler types, customers are very reluctant to act on a salesperson's promise that the value of an item will "definitely" justify the expenditure.

That's *Decision Making 101*. When the *perceived* value of a product or service exceeds the cost, it's easy to move forward with a decision. But, when the value being offered is unclear or doesn't justify the transaction, the answer will be, "No, thanks."

Customers Don't Want the Cheapest

Have you ever won a sale when your proposal was not the lowest priced alternative? Personally, I have experienced this scenario many times. What about the opposite—have you ever lost a deal where you were offering the lowest price, but for some strange reason, the customer opted to go with another supplier? Yep, me too.

I cut my teeth as a salesperson by selling big ticket software solutions in the high-tech marketplace. Potential buyers always complained about our price being too high. Come to find out, complaining about price is just part of the customer's role during a negotiation. Then one day, it occurred to me that the same decision makers who were always moaning about cost were surrounded by many other products and service options that were not the 'cheapest.' Technology giants like Oracle and Microsoft do not offer the cheapest software applications. IBM became a hundred-billion dollar company, but not by offering the absolute cheapest technology solutions. The Fortune 500 list of top performing companies is loaded with businesses who aren't selling the cheapest products.

As I pointed out in Chapter 1, most customers aren't looking to buy the absolute cheapest alternative. I bet you don't use the cheapest computer or live in the cheapest house. You don't eat the cheapest food or wear the cheapest clothes, right? You probably don't always choose the most expensive options, either. Instead, I find that most consumers gravitate to whichever solution gives them the biggest "bang for their buck."

The cost effectiveness of a proposed solution is critically important in terms of a consumer behavior. But, much like value, cost effectiveness is another area that is highly subjective. Something that seems like a good deal to one decision maker may not be perceived as cost effective by the next. That's because decision makers have different priorities, circumstances, and perspectives that affect their perception of your value.

If you offer the absolute cheapest product in a competitive situation, then your sales strategy may just be to try and convince customers that your proposed solutions will do *the same thing as other products, but for less money.* The more likely scenario is that your company's sales depend on some ability to differentiate your products and services from competitive offerings.

Thus, we're back to the idea of having enough perceived value to justify the cost. Remember my earlier illustration, the one where I cupped my hands to conceal an item that I claimed was valuable? If I had offered to reduce the price by ten percent, do you think people would have jumped at the chance to trade $18 for something that was still unknown? I bet they wouldn't have. Would an even further reduction in price have made a difference?

Granted, there are times in business when it's smart to offer discounts or incentives to spur sales. But, lowering your price just to create differentiation usually isn't a great sales strategy because you end up giving away profit margin without increasing the perceived value of your offering. Closing low margin deals is of little value to the company if you can't turn a profit.

If you want your deals to hinge on more than just price, then the focus of the sale must somehow shift to the other variable that will ultimately impact the decision—the customer's perception of your value. That becomes a function of your product or service's ability to accomplish specific decision objectives for the customer.

How Many Reasons Do Customers Have to Buy?

A customer's perception of your value is not some binary switch that gets flipped on or off. Rather, the value you offer is an intangible commodity that can increase or decrease based on the customer's perception of you, your products, and your company. Hence, the best sales strategy is the one that accumulates value throughout the sales process by addressing multiple facets of the customer's need.

For example, if it were completely up to you, how many reasons would you want customers to have to buy from you? It's a fair question. When I pose this question to live training audiences, the most common answer I hear back is, "One." Sometimes, people say, "At least one." I suppose that makes sense, because if a customer doesn't have at least one reason to buy your product or service, you probably won't make a sale. Regrettably, giving customers just one reason to buy from you is the wrong answer.

For years, traditional sales approaches have promoted the idea that in order to provide valuable solutions, you must first uncover a need. Salespeople are then sent out into their respective territories to *probe* for needs. We have since discovered that customers don't always know what they need. And even if they do recognize their own needs, they aren't always willing to openly share this information with a salesperson. As a result, probing for needs is a flawed strategy because it's not always as easy as it sounds.

Even when you successfully engage a new prospect and uncover a need, what then? Conventional wisdom would suggest that sellers should then address the customer's need by proposing one of your company's solutions. Ironically, that's where the rest of the train slides off the tracks.

One of my favorite parables that I started using to train salespeople way back in the mid-90's, is the now infamous water pump analogy. For training purposes, it's important to cause people to think outside the scope of their normal daily routines, in order to focus on two things: strategy and technique. So, for the next couple minutes, whether you are in the business of selling technology solutions, medical supplies, financial services, real estate, or manufactured goods, I want to divert you from thinking about your usual selling environment. Instead, I want you to imagine a scenario where you work as a salesperson for a fictitious company that sells pumps—water pumps.

Depending on where you are located geographically and the time of year, flooding can be a real problem. During the rainy season, for example, the foundation of a home can settle to the point where water starts seeping into the basement. Another unlucky scenario for a homeowner is to have a pipe burst because of sub-zero temperatures in the winter. A rapid spring-time thaw can be equally problematic, causing flooding headaches for even the most diligent homeowners.

Suppose a lead comes into our hypothetical water pump company, and you and I are selected to go on a joint sales call tomorrow to meet with a potential customer who is currently experiencing a flooding problem. Suppose also that you and I carve out a few minutes today to plan the call in advance. Do you ever strategize with colleagues or partners, or maybe with your boss before calling on a real live customer?

In our strategy session, the first thing we would ask ourselves is: What problem or issue is the homeowner trying to address? That's easy—they have a flooded basement. Done! We're ready to go meet with the customer, right? Not so fast! To understand why we are not yet prepared, let's fast forward out of our strategy session to anticipate what could happen during the actual sales call.

Seller: *(Knock...knock) "Hello, Mr. Customer, my name is Ted Jones with XYZ Pumps and this is my colleague, Susan Thompson. We are responding to your inquiry about water removal. How can we help?"*

Homeowner: *"Thanks for coming. Our basement is flooded."*

Seller: *"Well, let me tell you about our pumps!"*

For decades, we've had the notion drilled into our heads that sellers must first understand the customer's need. So, we try to find out what the customer wants or needs, usually by asking them. In this case, the customer is quick to share their problem—they have a flooded basement. Doesn't that sound like a need? Once we uncover the need, we have been conditioned to believe that's our queue to jump in and provide "solutions."

Here's the problem with basing your sales approach on outdated logic. After you've had this initial dialogue, how many reasons does the customer have to buy a water pump? The answer is, just one. And the reason? They have a flooded basement. But, if it was totally up to you, how many reasons would you want customers to have motivating them to purchase your product or service?

I can tell you with unflappable confidence that I would much rather my customers had three reasons to buy from me, instead of only one. For that matter, I would like customers to have six or seven reasons to buy from me, instead of only three. In fact, if it were totally up to me, I would just as soon customers had twelve, fifteen, or even twenty reasons to move forward with a purchase of my proposed solution.

Why? Identifying more reasons to buy your product or service usually translates into a greater sense of urgency on the part of customers to move forward with a purchase decision. Giving customers more reasons to buy from you also creates competitive separation. Case in point, if there are seven or eight reasons to buy from *you*, but only two or three to stay with a competitor, then you will be in a strong position to win the business. The opposite is true, where more reasons to go with a competitor means you lose any advantage. Lastly, giving customers more reasons to buy your product or service makes it easier for them to justify the expenditure.

Now, let's jump back into our pre-call strategy session in order to put this idea of expanding the customer's needs into practice. Once we understand that the customer is dealing with a water leak, we can easily expand the scope of the problem by asking ourselves the next logical question, which is: "Why might water in the basement be a problem for this homeowner? Unless you are a mind reader, there's no way to know exactly what the customer's hot buttons are prior to actually talking with them. But, since you and I would presumably be knowledgeable about our industry, we should be able to hypothesize in advance about how a flooded basement *might* impact the customer.

Frankly, the issue of flooding could have several implications. A simple water leak in the basement, for example, could affect the homeowner in lots of different ways, including:

1. structural damage
2. damage to personal property
3. mold or mildew
4. damage to furnace or the electrical system
5. unsanitary/health hazard
6. safety risk for children and pets
7. unwanted pests or insects
8. unable to use the space
9. damage to irreplaceable heirlooms
10. increased stress in the household
11. insurance issues
12. cost to clean up
13. time/hassle factor
14. resale value of home
15. unpleasant odor

Can you see how talking about the broader issue of having a "flooded basement" only scratches the surface of the customer's real challenges? What customers really want is to prevent structural damage, protect their personal property, eliminate mold and mildew, avoid damaging their furnace or electrical systems, etc. In fact, while some customers might be concerned about potential health risks, other homeowners will focus more on the hassle factor or cost to clean up the mess.

That's perfectly fine. As I said before, people buy for different reasons and different types of customers have different hot buttons and priorities. Nonetheless, recognizing that the underlying implications of an issue ultimately drives the customer's decision puts you in a stronger position to raise the customer's perception of the value you offer.

Watch what happens when we plug this thought back into our sample dialogue.

Seller:	*(Knock…knock) "Hello, Mr. Customer, my name is Ted Jones with XYZ Pumps and this is my colleague, Susan Thompson. We are responding to your inquiry about water removal. How can we help?"*
Homeowner:	*"Thanks for coming. Our basement is flooded."*
Seller:	*"Yes, we're getting lots of calls because of the recent storm. Could I ask, besides the obvious goal of getting the water out of your basement, what specifically are you most concerned about?"*
Homeowner:	*"Two things—I'm concerned about cost and possible structural damage to the foundation of my house."*

Asking, *"Besides the obvious goal of...?"*, is a brilliant way to open the floodgates of conversation (pardon the pun!). It's also not rhetorical, because it's absolutely fair for a salesperson to ask beyond "the obvious goal" to understand the full context of the problem at hand. Asking a rhetorical version of this question, like, "Why is flooding a problem for you?", puts you at risk of sounding naïve or inexperienced. If you are at all knowledgeable, then you should already know "why" flooding might be a problem for homeowners. Hence, by asking, *"Besides the obvious goal of_____, what specifically are you most concerned about?"*, it's predictable that most homeowners will mention one or more of the implications on our list.

When the customer in the sample dialogue responds by saying, "I'm concerned about cost and possible structural damage," this is valuable information for the seller, and a good start for identifying some of the more specific implications that are really driving the customer's need.

What's the likelihood that customers will name all fifteen implications on our list in response to your one question? I can tell you the chances of this happening are very slim. But, human nature is fairly predictable, so how many implications do you think most customers will bring up on their own? The answer is usually only one or two, and once in a while, three. So, who is going to bring up the other implications that might also be important to customers? If not you, then you leave the door wide open for a competitor be seen as a more valuable resource.

At the end of the day, I want customers to have multiple reasons to buy from me, and I want them to have a sense of urgency to move forward with a decision. I also want to make it as easy as possible for them to cost-justify the purchase. Bearing all of this in mind, it's fairly easy to expand the customer's needs and facilitate a more in-depth conversation, simply by raising additional implications, like:

Seller: *"Have you had flooding problems before?"*
"Is your basement used for storage only or is the water damaging personal property or impacting your family's living space?"
"Have you ever had mold or mildew in the house?"
"Where is the water in relation to the electrical box?"
"Are you sensing any unpleasant odors from that area?"
"Does your homeowner's policy cover this type of claim?"

With a few purposeful questions, the seller in this case can easily raise any number of potential implications (i.e. recurrence, personal property, inconvenience to the family, mold, mildew, safety, unpleasant odors, insurance) in the conversation that the customer may not otherwise have even thought about. Suddenly, the tally of important decision factors has increased from the initial two the customer mentioned (cost & structural damage) to as many as fifteen, if the seller were to raise all the implications noted above.

Frankly, if you are a bona fide expert in the field of dealing with flooded basements, you should absolutely be ready to bring up important decision issues that customers otherwise wouldn't think about. Would I barrage the customer with a litany of questions, or try to bring up all ten or fifteen implications while standing on the homeowner's doorstep? Probably not. But, I know that once the conversation starts rolling, there will be plenty of opportunities to broaden the dialogue.

Your Recipe for Success

Even if you haven't realized it yet, I imagine certain things in this chapter are starting to sound very familiar. Like any good recipe, in addition to identifying the right ingredients, to be successful, you must also be able to blend an array of different ingredients together into just the right mixture.

For example, the next time you prepare for a job interview, whether you are vying for a promotion within your existing company or competing for a new opportunity, you already know that the opening question in the interview will be some version of, "Tell me about yourself." At that point, we've said you have two choices—either to provide a dump of information about yourself (SPA), or focus on those things that might be most important to the hiring manager (PAS).

Though the hiring manager's primary goal may be somewhat obvious (wanting to hire the best person for the job), you can be sure there are several underlying and more specific implications that the interviewer is also hoping to satisfy by making a good choice. Let me show you what I mean in a quick revisit of the earlier interview dialogue.

Interviewer: *"Can you tell me a little about yourself?"*

Candidate: *"Well, since you have reviewed my work history already, I would add that I'm a hard working person with a solid track record. But, my guess is you may be looking for more than that to fill this position—perhaps some of the intangibles that don't always show up on a resume. For example, in addition to hiring someone who is knowledgeable and experienced, you might also want a person who can ramp up quickly and become productive as soon as possible. You may also be looking for someone who can blend with the current culture, but also bring new ideas and a fresh perspective to the team. As long as we're developing a wish list, you might also want someone with a positive attitude, who is self-motivated and customer-focused...(continued)."*

If the issues you raise during an interview are indeed important to the hiring manager, you are *"in like Flynn."* The candidate in this simple dialogue actually raises a host of decision factors including knowledge, experience, the learning curve, productivity, blending with the existing culture, and bringing a fresh perspective to the team. Certainly these "reasons to buy" would strike a chord with any manager who wanted the right person. As I said earlier, a salesperson who demonstrates that they are indeed customer-focused is much more valuable during a job interview (or sales call) than just claiming to be.

Don't be surprised if you are the only salesperson who takes the conversation down a customer-centric path. Most people will jump immediately into a self-indulgent diatribe and think they're doing well because they are answering the initial question that the interviewer asked.

Depending on the customer to fully articulate their own needs is bad strategy. Most will only mention some portion of the implications that actually impact their decision. That's okay; helping customers identify and understand their needs is one of the greatest opportunities we sellers have to provide value.

Sometimes, people push back on this idea, arguing that guessing at what customers might need puts a salesperson at risk of sounding presumptuous. Granted, you can't know exactly what customers need until you actually talk with them, but we're not exactly guessing here. If you specialize in a business that deals with a similar set of issues every day, if we use our industry knowledge along with a dash of common sense, couldn't we hypothesize as to what the customer's needs might be?

> "Helping customers identify and understand their needs is one of the greatest opportunities we sellers have to provide value."

Even though I haven't ever sold a water pump, it's easy to come up with a list of ten to fifteen implications of how a water leak could actually impact potential customers. The same logic applies to any value-based sale. For example, if you sell financial services, besides the obvious goal of making good investment decisions, what specifically are your customers trying to accomplish? Go ahead and ask about their specific goals. Don't be surprised, however, when customers only bring up some fraction of the implications on your list.

So, who's going to bring up the rest?

If you are prepared to facilitate your discussions with potential customers by proactively raising additional implications, be ready for the floodgates of conversation to burst wide-open. This is what I referred to earlier when I talked about *priming the pump*. The underlying lesson is simply this: when you raise valuable issues that a customer wouldn't necessarily have thought about on their own, they start to see you as a more valuable resource.

It's a credibility play. Once people begin to form the impression that you might be able to help them, customers are willing to share tons of information with any salesperson whom they perceive to be a valuable resource.

Do You Own an Umbrella?

Getting your arms around the customer's decision criteria is further complicated by the fact that people often speak in general terms, as opposed to articulating what they really need. This natural obtuseness creates another good opportunity for sellers who are prepared to facilitate more in-depth conversations.

To illustrate this phenomenon, here's a little exercise you can try. I often demonstrate this to audiences during live QBS training programs, and the scenario usually plays out the same way every time.

Basically, I pick out a face in the crowd and ask, "Do you own an umbrella?" Most people do. This is hardly an attempt to catch someone off-guard, as I'm just asking a simple question. With few exceptions over the years, the typical response is, "Yes, I do own an umbrella."

Out of curiosity, I ask a follow up question, "Why do you own an umbrella?" Again, there's no trick. I'm just asking *why* they own an umbrella.

"In case it rains," is the standard response.

This is where things get interesting. Watch what happens when I take the conversation to the next level by asking, "What is it about the rain that you are trying to avoid?"

"I don't want to get wet," the person will say. Fair enough. It makes total sense to me that someone would use an umbrella to protect themselves from getting wet.

But, what do you suppose happens to the value of the conversation when we dig even deeper, this time asking. "What is it exactly about getting wet that is undesirable?"

"I don't want to ruin my clothes."

Now we're getting somewhere. One of the reasons people own umbrellas is to protect their clothes (a nice silk scarf or leather jacket, for example) from getting ruined as a result of being caught in a downpour.

Other times, someone might say, "I don't want to catch a cold." That makes sense, too. Without an umbrella that protects you from getting soaked, you could get sick. By the way, if you got sick, you could miss work. And, if you miss work, you might lose an important sale and miss out on the commission. Can you see how the simple issue of 'getting wet' begets a whole trail of related implications?

Besides protecting your clothes and your health, there are plenty of other reasons people own umbrellas. A businessperson who wants to preserve a professional image, for example, probably would want to fend off inclement weather. For others, preventing the possibility of having to sit around all day in damp clothes is another big motivator. Still, other people use umbrellas to protect themselves from the sun, wanting to minimize the possible links between ultraviolet rays and skin cancer.

If you notice, the first person I ask always tells me that the reason they own an umbrella is, "in case it rains." Upon further analysis, we discover they were really trying to, "avoid getting wet." But, when we peel back the onion even further, we suddenly discover that what people *really* are trying to do is:

1. look their best
2. feel comfortable
3. protect their clothes
4. preserve a professional image
5. protect electronic devices
6. stay healthy
7. avoid sick days from work
8. not lose money
9. limit exposure to ultraviolet rays
10. move around freely during inclement weather

If you look back on the dialogue, it's not until the third layer of depth that we discover the true motivations behind why a person might want to own an umbrella. People don't buy umbrellas to "avoid getting wet." You don't take an umbrella into the shower, do you? Of course not. We are not averse to the idea of being wet. We just want to avoid getting soaked at certain inopportune times. Therefore, the value of an umbrella is more than just the avoidance of water, it's a whole list of potential motivators (implications).

One lesson to take away from this exercise is the realization that 'depth of conversation' is a salesperson's best friend. I'm not suggesting you should interrogate potential umbrella buyers. If you worked at a kiosk in the mall selling umbrellas, and you asked, "Why do you want an umbrella?", we know how most customers would answer—in case it rains. If you probed further, "Why, what happens if it rains?", you'd probably get some funny looks. If you pressed the issue by asking, "What are the real reasons you don't want to get wet?", rather than sharing their thoughts, customers would likely be turned off by your aggressiveness. People don't want to be probed for needs.

Some old-schoolers still defend the notion of *probing* for needs, saying that sellers must "drill down" to find out what is really driving the customer's decision. Frankly, this brings us to a crossroads in your professional development as a salesperson. If I sold umbrellas at a kiosk in the mall, I would probably ask potential customers this question, "Besides the obvious goal of staying dry, what specifically are you most concerned about?" I would be willing to bet my house that most customers will respond by mentioning one of the implications noted earlier. What's the likelihood they will bring up all ten? Again, it's very slim. Predictably, most customers will mention one or two, but I would be ready to facilitate a more valuable dialogue by raising additional implications that would otherwise not come up.

The actual value of your product or service doesn't change whether you have a detailed conversation or a superficial one. But, if the solutions you offer can address multiple issues and implications, and you know customers are not going to fully articulate their own needs, your value is closely linked to your ability to facilitate more in-depth conversations, which is very different than just probing customers about their needs.

Applying Your New Decision Logic

The question-based philosophy on needs development has shifted the paradigm from hoping customers will openly share all their needs with a salesperson, to a more proactive facilitation of what might be important to the customer. In QBS, our vision includes having sellers build credibility and value by actually helping customers recognize possible implications that would not have otherwise been considered. This is essentially what happens in every other profession. Whether you consult with a doctor, an attorney, an accountant, or an architect, as I said, you would want them to ask a series of intelligent questions first in order to then provide you with the best possible advice. Why should the sales profession be any different? In addition to providing solutions, helping customers understand the full extent of their needs has always been one of the salesperson's best opportunities to provide value.

Fortunately, the implementation and success of this approach comes with a price. I say "fortunately" because I know that most of my competitors aren't necessarily going to invest the time or effort to strengthen their position when dealing with customers. For me, if the difference between success and failure boils down to whoever is willing to put in the necessary time and effort, that gives me a distinct advantage.

> "If the difference between success and failure boils down to whoever is willing to put in the necessary time and effort, that gives me a distinct advantage."

It was great fun to win top salesman honors over multiple consecutive years. Success can be very motivating and rewarding, as many of you know. In addition to producing lots of revenue for my company, I was equally proud of my ability to ramp up quickly and become productive in a fraction of the time it took other people. There's no magic to doing this, it just requires some time and effort upfront, and a little strategic thinking.

If you would like to have a similar advantage, let me

encourage you to complete the same exercise I would do during my first week on the job if I accepted a position working for your company. I would create a physical document to serve as a "repository" of what issues might be important to prospective customers, along with a road map identifying the underlying implications of why each of those issues might be important. Knowing that decision makers buy for a variety of reasons, there is no better way to prepare yourself in advance of a sales call than to burn the issues and implications that might be important to customers into your top of mind memory. Of course, making a physical list also gives you a reference document to refer to and focus your thinking before your next conversation or meeting.

Build a Repository of Issues and Implications

Are you willing to make a one-time investment (of two hours) to kick start the rest of your sales career? That is approximately how much time it will take to complete this exercise. Honestly, nothing in my experience has proven to pay bigger dividends when facilitating needs development conversations with customers. If you do choose to invest in yourself, building a data base of possible issues and implications will change the way you interact with prospective customers. More importantly, it will change the way they perceive and interact with you.

If you buy into the notion of priming the pump, and you see the value of taking a leadership role when facilitating your needs development conversations with prospective customers, then you must prepare yourself in advance— much like the leader of a college debate team. How can you accomplish this in two hours?

Sample decision issues from selected industries.

Financial Services
Return on Investment
Safety of Principal
Growth of Capital
Risk
Diversification
Reporting
Market Updates
Estate Planning
Cash/Liquidity
Trust in Advisor
Access to Information
Inflation
Retirement Planning
Income Stream
Cost of Services
Confidentiality
Prompt Service
Integrity of Company
Consistent Performance
Tax Planning

Manufacturing
Materials Management
Inventory Turns
Growth
Fixed Costs
Shipping and Logistics
Innovation
Sales & Marketing
Strategic Planning
Customer Satisfaction
Security
Maintenance
Multiple Locations
Profitability
Labor Unions
Staffing
Quality Control
Communication
Information Technology
Global Markets
Research & Development

Real Estate
Location
Traffic Volume
Aesthetics
View
Noise
School Districts
Proximity to Healthcare
Local Job Market
Retail Options
Construction vs. Remodel
Broker Reputation
Timeframe for decision
Contingencies
Size of Family
Amenities,
Financing options
Pre – Qualification
Liquidity
Driving Distance to Work
Residential vs. Commercial

Technology
Availability
Performance
Scalability
Cost Effectiveness
Disaster Recovery
Manageability
Ease of Use
Interoperability
Customer Satisfaction
Upgradeability
Reliability
Maintenance
Support/Services
Time to Market
Company Viability
Industry Leadership
Data Integrity
Education/Training
Implementation
Remote Locations

Pharmaceutical
Clinical Efficacy
Trials/Studies
Exclusions
Possible Side Effects
Contra Indicators
Precaution Warnings
Drug Interactions
Multiple Indications
Cost Effectiveness
Alternative Generics
On Formulary
Paperwork Required
Managed Care
Ease of Use
Samples Available
Continuous Learning
Company Image
Rep. Availability
Patient Satisfaction
Legal Liability

Professional Services
Expertise
Available Resources
Timeframe for Decision
Quality
Experience
Job Security
Cost
Justification
Proximity
Location/Travel
Competitive Positioning
Employee Morale
Learning Curve
Legal Liability
Return on Investment
Project Scope
Requirements Definition
Future Needs
Peace of Mind
Time to Market

Figure 5.1

Start by making an inventory of possible business issues (or decision factors) that might be important to customers in your target market. (Repository is a just fancy word for data base.) Be sure to print a hard copy and keep an updatable version on your computer, as you will build onto this list as the next step. (Figure 5.1 shows examples from select industries).

Once you've constructed a comprehensive list of possible decision issues your customers might face, the next step is to broaden your value potential by creating a subordinate list of possible implications for each decision issue.

Just ask yourself, "Why might (issue) be important to a customer?" If you work in the financial services industry, for example, you might ask yourself, "Why might (return on investment) or (tax planning) be important to my customers?" You can ask customers, too. But, the magic of this technique is "arming" yourself in advance so that you can actually bring these implications up in the conversation, as opposed to always trying to coax and cajole it out of potential customers.

Make it your goal to create a physical list of ten implications for each decision issue. For example, return on investment might be important to a customer because of:

Sample Issue: Return on Investment

1. *Cash flow*	6. *Retirement planning*
2. *Tax Planning*	7. *Liquidity*
3. *Advisor confidence*	8. *Budgeting expenses*
4. *Investment buy/sell decisions*	9. *Peace of mind*
5. *College savings*	10. *Net worth*

Figure 5.2

Figure 5.3 Build a repository of decision issues and implications.

Issue: Return on Investment

1. *Cash flow*
2. *Tax Planning*
3. *Advisor confidence*
4. *Investment buy/sell decisions*
5. *College savings*

6. *Retirement planning*
7. *Liquidity*
8. *Budgeting expenses*
9. *Peace of mind*
10. *Net worth*

Issue: _____

1.
2.
3.
4.
5.

6.
7.
8.
9.
10.

Issue: _____

1.
2.
3.
4.
5.

6.
7.
8.
9.
10.

Issue: _____

1.   6.
2.   7.
3.   8.
4.   9.
5.   10.

Issue: _____

1.   6.
2.   7.
3.   8.
4.   9.
5.   10.

Issue: _____

1.   6.
2.   7.
3.   8.
4.   9.
5.   10.

Note to managers: QBS clients sometimes try to save time by assigning this task to a single person, with the idea that they could easily forward their repository list to everyone else on the team. I need to let you know that this is a mistake. Creating top-of-mind awareness for *what* issues might be important to customer and *why* those issues could be important, is a thought process that individual salespeople must create for themselves. Just reading email with an attached list of business issues and implications will not cause you to be perceived as a better resource to your customers.

Don't just make a list in your head, either. Invest the time to write it down, or create a worksheet on your computer, or flash-cards like the ones shown in Figure 5.3. Creating a permanent copy allows you to update the list over time as your product changes or your industry evolves. It also gives you a resource to glance at in preparation for important meetings, or even during live telephone conversations. I can promise you this. If you complete this exercise, you won't look at the actual document very often. As a byproduct of creating your physical list, you will also be burning these issues and implications into your memory.

For many years now I have been assigning the creation of this repository list as homework for QBS students, and I have yet to meet a salesperson who completed the exercise and didn't rave about their newfound success with customers. If you do the math on this, a repository of 20 decision issues with 10 implications for each issue suddenly creates 200 opportunities for a salesperson to provide value, which is very different than just randomly running around probing for needs.

While creating your repository list, you will also begin to notice that there is some overlap between the customer's issues and their corresponding implications, which is a good thing. You want this. Back in our earlier water pump analogy, for example, structural damage can affect the resale value of a home. Damaged personal property can also affect the overall cost of the customer's loss. Odor or mildew issues can similarly impact the livability of the home. The fact that these issues and implications are closely interrelated actually makes it easier for the strategic salesperson to navigate deeper, wider, and more strategic needs development conversations.

Again, how many reasons do you want customers to have to buy from you? Most sellers will spend way more than two hours chasing unqualified opportunities or deals that go away because there's little or no differentiation. Therefore, I say, why not invest those two hours upfront to put yourself in a position that will pay significant dividends for the rest of your sales career?

Chapter 6

Be More Strategic
with Your Sales Questions

Sellers have all been taught to ask lots of questions. But, just because a salesperson wants to ask questions, doesn't necessarily mean potential customers will open up and share with you.

In today's selling environment, it is possible to ask questions in a way that causes people to share lots of valuable information. It's also easy to ask questions that cause potential buyers to clam up and not share. The difference between the two scenarios is usually dictated by the strategy behind the questions you ask.

Some people are just smooth talkers, and they have a knack for navigating the flow of a sales conversation. You could say these people are born with the 'gift of gab.' Fortunately for the rest of us, there is also a *method* to proactively managing more productive business conversations. Not only is it possible to teach people how to facilitate more valuable interactions with customers, you can also implement a formula to easily repeat your success.

If we pull back the curtains on this (to use one of my favorite phrases) and we invest the time to understand the actual theory behind the questions you ask, a salesperson's goal shouldn't just be to pepper a prospect with questions. You also need to do something that will cause people to be more receptive to the questions you ask, to the point where they feel comfortable sharing information with you. Managing the types of questions being asked enables sellers to be more on target with their questions and also causes prospective customers to be more forthcoming with their responses.

From a sales perspective, the most common reason to ask questions is to gather information. To provide solutions, sellers must first understand the customer's needs, issues, goals, concerns, ambitions, objectives and priorities, as well as their timeframe for making a decision. Along the way, we also want to qualify potential opportunities to ensure we are making a good use of the customer's time, and our own. Some level of reconnaissance might also be needed, especially if you are the primary contact and are responsible for communicating account details with other members on your sales team.

This desire to collect information from customers has always taken center stage when it comes to needs development. *"Go out and probe for needs!"* has become a familiar battle cry within companies for many years. Consuming yourself with an inwardly-focused desire to gather information is unfortunately a classic example of how traditional sales thinking can actually inhibit your selling efforts, as "information gathering" is only one facet of an effective questioning strategy.

This idea of *being more strategic with your sales questions* is important because besides just collecting information, strategic questions can benefit a savvy salesperson in many other ways throughout the sales cycle. For example, a well placed strategic question is one of the best ways to pique the customer's interest, particularly early in the sales process when prospects are forming their initial impressions. Questions also provide one of the best ways for sellers to establish credibility with potential buyers. Used strategically, your ability to deliver the right question at the right time can also differentiate you from the competition, as well as increase the customer's sense of urgency to move forward with a decision. Questions can even be used to help cost-justify the purchase and overcome potential obstacles that pop up throughout the decision cycle. Therefore, if the only thing you do with questions is gather information, I will tell you that there is a huge upside opportunity to raise your sales effectiveness by leveraging the strategy behind the questions you choose to ask.

Information Gathering: The Downside

I agree that understanding a customer's needs, qualifying opportunities, and communicating with others who also need to be in the loop is an important part of many sales roles. To fulfill these objectives, sellers must absolutely gather information from prospective customers. There's just one catch. Soliciting information from potential buyers often feels (to them) like a self-serving act on the part of the salesperson. Sure, you're trying to make a sale, but what's in it for them?

I'm not suggesting that you should stop gathering information about your sales opportunities. However, I can show you how to ask questions more effectively, in a way that will lower a decision maker's natural defenses and engage more prospects in more productive conversation. You accomplish this by asking questions strategically, in a manner that causes customers to recognize that sharing important information with a salesperson actually gets them closer to achieving their objectives.

The truth of the matter is, if someone doesn't *want to* share with you, then it doesn't matter what you ask. That's why it's not just about asking questions. Fortunately for salespeople, the opposite is true—the moment a customer begins to see you as a valuable resource, they start helping you to help them. The challenge is getting over that initial hump in the conversation, so customers have an incentive to open up.

The Fallacy of Open-Ended Questions

Are you familiar with the traditional labeling of questions as being "open" or "closed-ended?" By definition, a closed-ended question is one that can be answered with a single word or phrase, like a simple yes or no. For example, "Mr. Customer, do you currently own a home?" Closed-ended questions are not limited to yes/no responses, however. A salesperson could just as easily have asked, "How many employees are in your company?" While the person could choose to elaborate with more details, this is still a closed-ended question that can be appropriately answered with a single word or phrase, like, "Seventy-three."

An open-ended question, therefore, is a question that cannot be appropriately answered with a single word or phrase.

The very first sales course I ever attended was the old Xerox course, called Professional Selling Skills (PSS). One of the main themes that was drilled into our heads during the training was, "If you want to *open* a dialogue with prospective customers, then you should ask open-ended questions."

Xerox pretty much wrote the book on sales training back then. Consequently, kicking your sales conversations off with open-ended questions has been the prevailing advice offered in most of the sales training courseware over the last thirty years. At first glance, the strategy appears valid—opening customer conversations with open-ended questions seemed logical enough. What salesperson doesn't want to "open" a productive exchange with potential buyers? So, the Xerox training along with many other courses have taught sellers to initiate their sales conversations with open-ended questions like:

Seller: *"Mr. Customer, what's the biggest issue you currently face?"*
"What are your goals and objectives for the next five years?"
"What keeps you awake at night?"

These are classic examples of *open probes*, as Xerox called them. Since my initial Xerox training, I have attended countless training courses and read dozens of sales books that all tout the same philosophy—if you want to open a dialogue, start with open-ended questions. I attempted this approach during my early years in sales, but starting with open-ended questions never quite made sense to me. In hindsight, asking open-ended questions to try and "open" a dialogue was one of the reasons I struggled so much early in my sales career.

Salespeople are still being taught to "open" their conversations with open-ended questions, even though it is widely acknowledged that prospects are reluctant to open up and share information with someone they yet don't know or trust.

Next time you receive a cold call at home, and the salesperson opens the dialogue by saying, "Hi, Mr. Jones, this is Joe

Smith with Equitable Real Estate Life Insurance Mortgage Company, what are your financial goals and objectives for the next five years?" Are you likely to open up and share your long term financial goals with a total stranger? I doubt it.

As our society grows increasingly more cautious and skeptical of people we don't yet know or trust, sellers should no longer assume prospects will "open up" just because you want to ask a few broad, sweeping sales questions. In fact, asking for too much information, too soon is more likely to seem invasive and inappropriate. Customers are more likely to think, "You don't have enough credibility to ask me that question." Or, "Why would I share that information with a total stranger?"

Sellers Start with Near-Zero Credibility

As a skeptical buyer myself, it has always been my view that sellers start with near-zero credibility. Customers don't actually despise salespeople, however. Instead, most decision makers rely on vendor salespeople for ideas, information, vision into the future, and for solutions. But, as I said earlier, customers simply aren't going to depend on every salesperson who comes calling.

> "Decision makers depend on vendor representatives—for ideas, information, vision into the future, and potential solutions."

Like it or not, we sellers inherit the prejudices and negative baggage from all of the other salespeople who have previously called on the customer but didn't neccessarily provide value. And, unless you do something to separate yourself from the stereotypes customers harbor toward an unproven salesperson, prospects will assume you offer little or no value until you prove otherwise. That's what I mean by starting with near-zero credibility.

The current level of standoffishness from decision makers creates an interesting paradox, where prospective buyers are reluctant to share their needs with a salesperson who has not yet established their credibility, but the only way to establish credibility is to somehow engage potential customers in a productive conversation about their needs.

So, how can sellers break this cycle? How can you establish your own credibility, enough to engage potential buyers early in the sales process? There are three options a salesperson has to try and establish credibility with prospective customers. One option is to leverage existing relationships. If you know people who can introduce you to key people within your target accounts, then you may have a red carpet directly into the decision maker's office. Leveraging existing relationships is especially good for getting deeper, wider, and more strategic within existing customer accounts. The bigger challenge, however, is finding a way to establish credibility with potential customers where no relationship currently exists.

Another option, and the most common way sellers attempt to gain credibility, is by claiming it—generally in the form of an elevator pitch. When a customer or hiring manager says, "Tell me about yourself (or product)," most sellers do exactly that— they spew information about themselves, their company, or their product in the hopes of boosting their credibility and engaging prospects in a mutually beneficial business conversation.

I talked about the pitfalls of trying to claim your own credibility back in Chapter 2. Remember, telling about themselves is what most people do during a job interview. Given that propping yourself up can sound presumptuous or arrogant, trying to proclaim your own greatness can also cause cautious customers to retreat even further. As a consumer yourself, when a salesperson claims to offer the greatest product since sliced bread, do you accept their word at face value?

The third option for establishing credibility is to *earn* it. Real life experiences, and having completed several semesters at the school of hard knocks, have taught me to believe that credibility is not something that can just be claimed. In today's business climate, where buyers are more cautious and standoffish than ever before, sellers have to "earn their own stripes" in every account. It's worth noting that credibility must also be demonstrated on an individual basis, which requires a proactive effort on the salesperson's part to do something that will cause decision makers to perceive you as a truly valuable resource.

If we agree that credibility must be earned, the question now becomes: what can sellers do to establish more credibility with prospective customers, as early in the sales process as possible?

Use Diagnostic Questions to Establish Credibility

Back when I was a rookie salesperson first learning the ropes, it didn't take long to discover that prospects weren't necessarily eager to share information with someone they didn't know. This created a huge problem for me since I was new to the company and the territory. While the prevailing philosophy at the time revolved around this idea that open-ended questions would somehow open the dialogue, it quickly became apparent that asking highly invasive questions was causing prospects to shut down rather than open up. Trying to impress people with an elevator pitch about my product or company wasn't helping either. Now what to do?

Under normal sales conditions, time is of the essence. When making cold calls, for example, sellers usually have a brief window of time, during which you had better pique the customer's interest and establish your own credibility, or whatever window of opportunity you have will quickly close. Herein lies the challenge; figuring out some method for piquing the customer's interest and establishing your own credibility (both), within a relatively small amount of time.

Logic finally triumphed over tradition and I decided to stop approaching customers with the same canned, open-ended questions that were turning them off. Instead, I thought...*if asking for too much too soon was causing a problem, I wonder what would happen if I tried taking a few baby steps on the way to accomplishing the larger objective?* Are you familiar with the adage, "You must first learn to walk before you can run?"

After experimenting with different types of questions, I began to notice that customers responded much more "openly" when I took a softer, more considerate approach, versus aiming for the jugular and asking something like, "What's the biggest issue you currently face?" This idea of earning the right to engage has since evolved into one of the foundational philosophies within the QBS methodology. As a result, we now spend a fair amount of time "undoing" the mindset of a previous generation of salespeople and replacing it with contemporary logic that will enable you to have more effective needs development conversations. The specific technique is called *Diagnostic Questions.*

Scope, Focus, and Disposition

In Question Based Selling we don't refer to questions as being open or closed-ended, mostly because those labels are neither current nor robust enough to capture the true strategic value of a well-placed sales question. I'll say it again—if all you're doing with questions is gathering information, then you have a huge upside opportunity to leverage questions to generate more initial interest, create competitive separation, increase a customer's sense of urgency, and cost-justify the decision—not to mention establishing your credibility with potential clients. That's why, in QBS, we focus more on the conversational dynamics aspect of using sales questions and techniques to invoke predictable and consistent responses from customers.

Who's in control of the questions you ask? You are, right? Then, I can tell you right now that your ability to manage the *Scope*, *Focus*, and *Disposition* of your questions will have a direct impact on how productively people respond. Of course, being aware of what types of questions you ask is very different than just randomly probing for needs.

Our study of strategic questioning begins with the concept of *Scope*. Specifically, let's zero-in on the strategy of *narrowing the scope* of your questions in order to establish more credibility sooner.

The *Scope* of a question refers to its broadness, or narrowness. Like closed-ended questions, questions that are narrow in scope can easily be answered with a single word or phrase. These questions tend to be less invasive, and, because you are asking about specific data points, they are easy for salespeople to ask, and easy for customers to answer. Narrowing the scope of your questions essentially becomes our stepping stone strategy for kicking off your needs development conversations. Once you earn the right to get into more depth, then you can easily broaden the scope of your questions and probe more deeply into the customer's issues and concerns.

Managing the "Scope" of Your Questions

Let's put this technique of managing the *Scope* of your questions in the appropriate context. Frankly, in today's selling environment, you shouldn't just pick up the telephone and barrage prospects with questions of any kind. Especially on your initial call, the first thing customers want to know is who you are and why you're calling. These conversations need to have a sense of purpose, presumably because you are calling for some reason that is relevant and valuable to the customer. I will talk more about how to open sales calls in a purposeful manner later. For now, let's agree that in most sales conversations, there will be an opportunity to ask questions at some point. The opportunity could come at the 15-second mark in your conversation, or after a few minutes, but at some point in the call, there will be an opportunity for you to ask questions about the customer's situation or potential needs.

My first needs development question is almost always the same. At the appropriate time in the conversation, I simply say, *"Mr. Customer, can I ask you a couple specifics about (blank)?"* Simply fill in the blank with something that is relevant to them, and this question is sure to generate a mini-invitation.

In golf terms, this question is an absolute gimme. Unless you are dealing with the type of person who isn't going to talk with you no matter what, if you are calling for a purposeful reason, securing the customer's permission to proceed instantly makes a salesperson's job easier because it lowers the customer's natural defenses. Of course, this paves the way for you to ask "a couple specifics" about their situation.

The best way to show you how this technique actually works is to create a real-life scenario. If you were an independent life insurance agent, for example, opportunities for needs development would arise at some point during your client conversations. Once you secure the customer's permission to proceed, you simply ask a series of specific *Diagnostic Questions* to better understand the customer's situation. The actual conversation might go something like this:

Industry: Life Insurance

Salesperson: *"Ms. Customer, can I ask you a couple specifics about your current insurance coverage?"*
- *Do you currently own a life insurance policy?*
- *Was it provided by your employer or purchased separately?*
- *Is your existing life insurance whole life or term?*
- *How long has your current policy been in force?*
- *How many people are in your immediate family?*
- *When did you last review your insurance needs?*

See figure 6.1 for additional industry examples.

There's no need to shy away from being respectful or polite, as we definitely want to make good use of the customer's time. In most cases, this approach of taking a couple baby steps on the way to the larger needs development conversation is welcomed by customers as a refreshing change from those sellers who

Figure 6.1 Sample diagnostic questions for different industries.

Industry: **Software**

Salesperson: *"Mr. Customer, can I ask you a couple specifics about your current IT platform?"*

- Is your current IS environment centralized or distributed?
- What's your primary operating system for applications?
- Do you develop applications in house or buy packaged software?
- How much of your programming effort is object oriented?
- How many users do you support?
- In how many locations?

Industry: **Real Estate**

Salesperson: *"Mrs. Customer, can I ask you a couple specifics about your real estate objectives?"*

- Are you interested in purchasing an existing home or building?
- Do you need to sell your current home?
- How long have you lived there?
- How many people in your family?
- When was the last time your home was appraised?
- Can I ask what business are you in?

Industry: **Manufacturing**

Salesperson: *"Can I ask you a couple specifics about your current operations environment?"*

- How much of your production occurs in the main plant?
- Do you use prefab materials or fabricate your own components in-house?
- Approximately how many suppliers are involved?
- Where is the product warehoused once completed?
- What kind of inventory system do you have in place?
- Supporting how many SKU numbers?

Figure 6.1 Sample diagnostic questions (continued).

Industry: **Healthcare**

Salesperson: *"Dr. Smith, Can I ask you a couple specifics about your current patient services?"*

- How many clinics do you support?
- Are they automated with hand held devices?
- Does patient data update real time or at end-of-day?
- How many patients do you care for per month?
- What's the mix of long term care vs. short term?
- Do you use third party billing or handle those functions in-house?

Industry: **Office Furniture**

Salesperson: *"Ms. Customer, can I ask you a couple specifics about your current facilities environment?"*

- How much of your furniture is cubicles versus free standing desks and chairs?
- Is your office decor traditional or contemporary?
- Do you prefer steel or a wood-grain finishes?
- How many employees in your company?
- Residing at how many locations?
- Do you own the office space or lease it?

Job Interview Scenario

Diagnostic Questions one might ask during an interview:

Candidate: *"Can I ask you a couple specifics about the open sales position?"*

- Are you creating a new position or replacing someone?
- To whom does the position report?
- How many people are on that person's team?
- How many other people are interviewing for this job?
- What percentage of the job is business development versus an account management role?

aggressively probe for needs. Especially in today's buying climate, buyers are no longer willing to endure the traditional grilling from an over-eager salesperson.

Notice that each of the diagnostic questions in the sample are intentionally narrow in *Scope*. This enables you to gather a series of relevant data points about the status of the opportunity in a small window of time (generally within sixty seconds). This is significant because the first minute of your needs development conversation represents the single best opportunity sellers have to establish credibility with potential customers. Granted, this initial window is not your only chance to establish credibility, but it is by far the best opportunity to make a favorable impression, especially when you are selling yourself.

Potential buyers are always forming impressions, right? Do people form impressions based on statements a salesperson makes? Sure they do. But, customers also base their impressions on questions you ask. With that in mind, let me offer up a quick lesson in human nature: If you can demonstrate an ability to ask a series of relevant and intelligent questions, customers will automatically form the impression that you are knowledgeable in each of these areas.

My goal here isn't to earn a Ph.D. in less than sixty seconds. I just want people to give me the benefit of the doubt and begin to form a positive first impression that will help separate me from other sellers the customer has previously dismissed. The goal is simply to demonstrate to potential buyers that you are indeed a valuable resource.

Asking about specific data points keeps your questions short, which minimizes your risk of sounding too invasive. Of course, the information you gather helps guide the conversation and transition into more depth. The best part is, there is no downside to initiating your needs development conversation by asking a series of specific diagnostic questions. If you were selling life insurance, for example, you would want to know a few specific facts about the customer, like if the prospect currently owned a policy, was it provided as part of their employee benefits package, and whether the policy was term insurance or whole life?

Sometimes a student in one of my classes will ask, "Can't you just ask people about their current life insurance goals?" Sure, you can ask prospective customers whatever you like. And, if they are the type of person who is willing to share information with a perfect stranger, you're golden. But, that scenario is becoming rarer and rarer. As a result, asking for too much too early in the conversation has become one of the quickest

> "Asking for too much too early in the conversation has become one of the quickest ways to cause people to close up and not share."

ways to cause people to close up and not share, which is the opposite of our objective in needs development.

In addition to boosting your credibility, this technique of asking diagnostic questions is also a good way to pique the prospect's interest. Within a short time window, asking relevant questions about the customer's current situation causes potential buyers to start thinking about details. Has their family situation changed, such that their insurance needs are suddenly different? Especially if they haven't reviewed their existing coverages in a while, getting customers to think about specifics creates all kinds of opportunities for you to expand the needs development conversation.

Again, using diagnostic questions at the beginning of your needs development conversations is purely a stepping-stone strategy to get into more depth. If you succeed in kicking the needs development conversation off in a non-threatening manner, gathering valuable information that will direct the dialogue, establishing your own credibility as a valuable resource, and earning the right to expand the conversation, it then becomes very easy to *broaden the scope* of the conversation in order to understand the customer's true goals and objectives.

Create a Bank of Diagnostic Questions

People are sometimes surprised to hear me say I'm not a fan of pre-call scripting. Don't get me wrong; you should absolutely be well prepared before making customer calls. It's just not realistic to document a verbatim script prior to each and every customer conversation. Honestly, most sellers end up just thinking of whatever questions they want to ask on the fly.

My advice to salespeople is to prepare yourself by completing a one-time exercise, where you essentially establish a bank of possible diagnostic questions that could be used when kicking off your needs development conversations. There must be twenty or thirty data points you would want to know about a customer if you were given carte blanche to ask whatever you wanted.

The goal of this exercise is to totally prepare yourself one time, in order to then have a reusable repository of diagnostic questions you can use on a continuing basis. To me, this exercise isn't really optional. If you want customers to perceive you as a valuable resource, then you should absolutely have a clear understanding of the specifics you want to ask before you actually contact the customer. This investment on the front end also creates an ongoing asset that will pay dividends on your future sales conversations.

"Focus" on Escalating Your Questions

Once you understand how to narrow the *Scope* of your questions to initiate a more productive needs development conversation, it's time to escalate the *Focus* of your questions to get into more depth. Every question you ask has a strategic *Focus*, where you are either asking about the *status* of an opportunity, *issues* that a customer might be facing, the resulting *implications* of those issues, or you ask questions that focus on possible *solutions* for moving forward. Hence, the second strategic attribute that sellers have an opportunity to manage is the *Focus* of your questions.

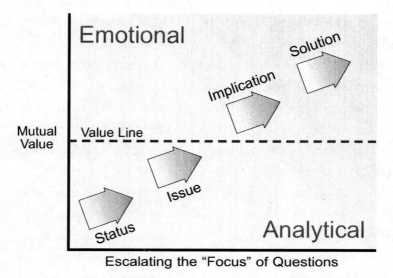

Fig 6.2 Escalate the value of your sales conversations by escalating the strategic *Focus* of your sales questions.

In the lower left of the diagram, *Status Questions* are valuable tools used to gather (or verify) pertinent facts about the customer—relevant data points that will help to guide the conversation. These questions should seem familiar, as we just talked about the strategy of kicking off your needs development conversations with a series of short answer diagnostic questions that *Focus* on the *status* of the opportunity. *Status Questions* are intentionally narrow in scope, which provides sellers with a non-threatening way to establish credibility, and a starting point for needs development. It's important to realize, however, that *Status Questions* are lowest in mutual value, as shown on the left-hand axis in Figure 6.2.

Kicking off your needs development conversations by asking about the status of an opportunity is a terrific strategy. However, questions like, "How many people in your company?", or, "Was your existing software purchased or developed in-house?", are low in *mutual value* because the customer isn't receiving any benefit. They already know the answers to these questions. Sellers must, therefore, escalate the value of the conversation by asking questions that focus on the customer's more important decision issues.

Every purchase is ultimately driven by whatever decision issues are most important to the customer. Are they trying to increase revenues, motivate employees, meet new compliance standards, or reduce maintenance costs? The only way to actually provide valuable solutions is to identify and address the customer's concerns. That's where *Issue Questions* come in.

Issue Questions are more valuable than *Status Questions* (Figure 6.2) because they represent the first real stage of problem solving. Once you've kicked the conversation off in a non-threatening manner, gathered valuable information, established your own credibility, and earned the right to get into more depth, it's time to broaden the *Scope* of your questions and focus on the customer's actual goals and objectives. You can literally watch customers perk up and lean forward in their chairs when you escalate the conversation from *Status Questions* to *Issue Questions*.

The transition to *Issue Questions* is relatively simple. In fact, we touched on it briefly back in Chapter 5. Let's play out the dialogue so you can see how the conversation actually flows.

Salesperson: *"Can I ask you a couple specifics about your current insurance coverage?"*

Customer: *"Sure."*

Salesperson: *Do you currently own a life insurance policy?*
Provided by employer or purchased separately?
Is your existing insurance whole life or term?
How long has your current policy been in force?
How many people are in your immediate family?
When did you last review your insurance needs?

Salesperson: *"Well, let me ask you this—besides the obvious goal of protecting your family in the event of an unexpected death, what specifically are you wanting to accomplish by having a life insurance policy?"*

Once you earn the right to get into more depth, it's easy to tee an issue up for discussion by saying, "To what extent is (*issue*) important?" That's the value of *Issue Questions*.

The syntax of this question is particularly interesting. In

addition to raising a valid issue for discussion, asking, "To what extent…," also broadens the *Scope* of your questions. This signals to customers that it's time for them to respond with full sentences and paragraphs, as opposed to just specific data points.

If you are wondering what issue to start with, try asking, "To what extent is your (current situation) growing or changing?" The issue of 'growth or change' offers a valuable starting point in most industries because it is a relevant topic with virtually everyone you call on. Just fill in the blank with something you know to be relevant to them. For example, executives might focus on how growth or change is affecting the budget, while a department head might be fully absorbed with how certain changes are affecting their production line. Even when selling to individuals, it's perfectly acceptable to ask, "To what extent is your family's insurance needs growing or changing?"

Escalate Further to Identify Implications

If you get nothing else out of this book, it's critical to understand that just uncovering issues that are important to customers is not enough. You must further escalate your conversations to *Focus* on "why" those issues are indeed important. Otherwise, the issues you identify don't really mean anything. You must also understand the implications of why certain decision criteria is important to the customer.

For example, if you say to a doctor, "I feel sick," the doctor doesn't yet have enough information to properly diagnose your problem. When someone says they feel sick, they could mean anything from heartache to the flu. Likewise, if a customer says they are growing by ten percent year-over-year, that doesn't tell you whether their growth is coming from increased revenues, geographic expansion, new product lines, widening distribution channels, or something else.

To offer solutions, sellers must understand how a given issue actually impacts the customer. The implications of the problem or issue are ultimately what provide buyers with the motivation and justification needed to move forward with a purchase. Again, how many reasons do you want customers to have to buy from you? Me, I want potential buyers to recognize as much value as possible in what I offer. Therefore, my goal in needs development is to broaden the customer's thinking in a way that expands their decision criteria to include implications they wouldn't necessarily think up on their own. This is easily accomplished by asking *Implication Questions*.

For example, when you ask, "To what extent is your business growing or changing?", the customer might respond by saying, "We expect to grow about six percent this year," In order to understand how growth might be impacting their business, I could ask any number of Implications Questions like:

Seller: *"How does that impact your overall marketshare?"*
"Any plans to open new stores?"
"Are you entering new markets?"
"What does your pipeline for new products look like?"
"How will that affect current staffing levels?
"In what ways will this impact your supply chain?"
"At what point will you need more physical space?"
"How does this compare with the competition?"
"How will this expansion affect your role?"
"Do any of these changes affect you personally?"

In Chapter 5, I suggested an exercise where you build a repository list of potential business issues—and under each issue, create a list of possible implications. The sample list above has ten implications that could easily be used to expand the conversation or at least better understand the issue of "growth and change." Is it possible that customers might raise some fraction of these implications on their own? Sure, but who's going to bring up the rest? If not you, then you leave the door wide open for the competition to come in and identify opportunities you may not be addressing.

Would I rattle off all ten implication questions every time the issue of growth came up? Of course not. But, I would be ready to raise whichever implications I thought might be important based on how the exchange was flowing. Once you work through the conversation about growth and change, using this escalation model, it's easy to then transition to another important issue.

This strategy is pretty straightforward. Simply raise a decision issue for discussion, and then expand the needs development conversation by asking about *implication, implication, implication.* Raise another issue, and then explore *implication, implication, implication.* Issue...*implication, implication, implication*...and so on. Each time a new issue is raised, you simply escalate the conversation to better understand the prospect's thoughts, feelings, and concerns regarding that particular topic.

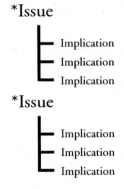

How many issues and implications should you raise? That will largely depend on the customer and the natural flow of the conversation. The most important part of this strategy is preparation. If you have armed yourself with a clear picture of *what* issues might be important to your customers, and you are able to facilitate a conversation about *why* those issues are important (i.e. implications), using this escalation strategy will change the way you interact with customers, and it will also change the way customers perceive you.

Global Questions are Valuable Tools

Global Questioning is another Question Based Selling technique I developed to further escalate your needs development conversations. Even when people do share information, most tend to share fractionally. If you're talking with your best friend in the world, and you want them to share more information, all you have to do is say, "Tell me more." When forging new relationships with potential customers, however, commanding people to give you more information is a strategic miss. Thus, a *Global Question* is a question-based tool you can use to say, "Tell me more," without sounding like you are giving a command.

If you notice, global questions contains no subject. Instead, they build on the context of the existing conversation. Examples of global questions include:

Seller: *"Like what?"*
"What else?"
"How do you mean?"
"What happens next?"
"How would that work?"

Try one of these. The next time someone says something to you (or, asks you a question), try responding with a *Global Question*. You will be shocked at how easy it is to further escalate your conversations and get into more depth.

Do people like it when you show interest in what they are trying to communicate? The answer is, yes, absolutely! *Global Questions* are intended (and usually taken) as subtle compliments. They demonstrate that you are indeed interested in what the other person has said or asked, as you are essentially inviting them to please continue. In terms of conversational dynamics, *Global Questions* act like a reverse mini-invitation, where you are now inviting the customer to share more.

Global Questions are not only easy to deliver, they are also some of the most productive questions you can ask—especially when you are trying to encourage prospects to open up and talk about the underlying aspects of a problem or an upcoming decision.

Use Solution Questions to Secure Next Steps

Sometimes a needs development conversation only lasts a couple of minutes. Other times, a more in-depth review of the customer's needs can span several hours. Mostly it depends on the type of sale and the particular customer situation. However, once you understand what a customer wants to accomplish, it's time to escalate your questions one more time, to *Focus* on the desired results that will come from procuring the right solution. This is where *Solution Questions* become valuable closing tools, to secure the next appropriate step in the sales process (Figure 6.2).

Solution Questions help to balance your needs development conversations. While we want prospects to have a sense of urgency to move forward, we are not trying to overwhelm them with the magnitude of a problem. Instead, we want customers to be excited and enthusiastic about actually solving the problem, as they realize that positive emotions like satisfaction and relief are just around the corner from their current pain, frustration, or concern.

Escalating your questions to focus on possible solutions is just as easy as the other transitions. Basically, you summarize the customer's requirements and then suggest an appropriate next step in the decision process. Here's a quick hypothetical.

Salesperson: *"Mr. Customer, if (issue), (issue), and (issue) are all important to your business because of (implication) and (implication), would it make sense for us to (insert appropriate next step)?"*

What should you suggest as the next step in your sales process? That depends on what you are selling. The appropriate next step might be a technical meeting, an executive briefing, or if you sell to individuals, the next step in the decision could be to schedule a follow up meeting with the prospect's spouse. The appropriate next step might even be to move forward toward a purchase.

Another type of *Solution Question* is to simply ask customers to visualize the perfect solution.

Salesperson: *"Mr. Prospect, in your mind, what would the ideal solution to this problem look like?"*

Once potential buyers perceive you as a valuable resource, they will absolutely want to confide in you regarding their problems, issues, and concerns. They will also want you to recommend or agree to the appropriate next steps. That's why it is critical to have a strategy that escalates the *Focus* of your needs development questions—first earning the right to engage, then identifying multiple opportunities to provide value, and finally, closing on next steps. If you can consistently accomplish these goals, you will differentiate yourself from the other salespeople who are still stuck in the traditional approach of asking highly invasive and probative questions.

Chapter 7

Selling Intangibles and Cost Justification

The value proposition of every product or service is highly intangible. Even if you sell tangible goods, the value you offer must still be conceptualized by potential buyers, and the benefits must be great enough to justify the cost of your solution.

What if you could increase the value of your offering merely by causing customers to perceive more benefits? Besides separating yourself from the competition, selling the intangible aspects of your solution is the best way to tip purchase decisions in your favor.

Everyone knows that in order to make a sale, the value of a product or service must be great enough to justify the cost. Back in Chapter 5, however, I made the point that there is no such thing as *actual value*. Why? Because the value of your solution is increased or diminished by the customer's perception of how much it will help them. Causing customers to perceive greater value from your offerings than a competitor's, and enough value to justify a purchase, becomes an important sales skill and one that must be developed.

Are the products you sell tangible or intangible? If we use product specifications to define tangibility, the answer might boil down to whether or not you can physically touch the product. If so, then it must be a tangible item. Someone who sells computer equipment, for example, could rightly assume that a laptop computer is a tangible product. Not only can you touch it, you can place it on your lap and tap on the keys. A salesperson who reps medical supplies can reach the same conclusion regarding their new line of IV pumps. If you can physically bring one of the pumps into an operating room and hand it to a doctor, then it must be a tangible item.

Selling services is a different story. You can't physically touch a dozen hours of consulting time or pull them out of a briefcase to show a customer during a sales call. Yet, consulting time is still a valuable item. Insurance products are similarly intangible. Lots of people buy life, auto, and homeowner's insurance, but besides a hard copy of the contract with all its terms and conditions, you cannot hold the actual insurance in your hand.

Some people believe that selling intangibles is more difficult than selling tangible goods, mostly because customers can't actually touch the product. I'll grant you that selling intangibles is definitely a conceptual sale, where benefits must be perceived by customers in order to register value. The fact that a salesperson or company believes their product *is* valuable is not enough to convey value, however. Somehow, this belief must be transferred to the customer.

But, guess what? Even if the product you sell is tangible or touchable, the value proposition of the item is still highly intangible. This creates an interesting paradox—though you can hold tangible items in your hand, the real value that comes from purchasing them is still highly intangible.

For example, we agreed that a laptop computer is a tangible item, right? But, while you can definitely hold a laptop in your hands (or on your lap), you can't actually touch its true value. Think about it. Why are laptop computers valuable? Different types of users have different hot buttons, but speaking for myself, my laptop is valuable because it is convenient, it enables to me to be more productive, and it allows me to stay connected while I'm away from the office. Have you ever stopped to consider that you can't actually touch convenience, productivity, or the value of staying connected with your business? You might be able to measure the degree to which productivity has increased, but you still cannot hold it in your hand. Other intangible benefits of a laptop computer, including increased mobility, reliability, ease of use, or the ability to play computer games on long flights, are also valuable, but you can't hold any of those things in your hand either.

The same principle applies to most sales, whether you sell real estate, manufactured goods, telecommunications, or medical supplies. Take residential real estate. It's a tangible item, right? You certainly can see and touch the house, the yard, and other physical characteristics of the property. But, it's important to realize that most people who buy residential real estate aren't looking at physical characteristics only. They're usually just as interested in intangibles like location, usefulness, aesthetic beauty, spaciousness, growth potential, return on investment, quality of schools, and the view of the backyard from the kitchen window.

The value proposition of a more sophisticated product like a clinical IV pump in medical sales is just as intangible.

Although medical devices are certainly tangible items, physicians don't care that much about product specifications. What they really care about are things like ease of use, clinical efficacy, patient comfort, availability of product, cost effectiveness, possible complications, reimbursement, liability, and seamless integration with other devices.

> "Even if you sell tangible goods, the true value proposition of those items comes from an array of highly intangible benefits that must be perceived."

Everyday products like tooth brushes, breakfast cereal, automobile tires, or a nice pair of Italian loafers have similarly intangible value propositions. You can't actually touch the value of fresh breath, a healthy diet, keeping your family safe while driving in the rain, or feeling stylish all the way to the ground. Hence, even if you sell tangible goods, the true value proposition of those items comes from an array of highly intangible benefits that must be perceived by interested buyers.

If you think about it, the whole concept of *Selling Yourself,* especially *in today's competitive marketplace,* is extremely intangible.

Competitive Intangibility

You know what's weird? Companies invest millions of dollars to position their products, and salespeople work extremely hard to differentiate their respective value propositions, but most customers still can't articulate exactly why they prefer one solution over another. For some reason or another, after considering the alternatives, the decision maker just felt more comfortable with one solution over the competition.

The vendor of choice in a competitive situation may not even have a distinct advantage. I've been involved in numerous sales scenarios where more than one vendor proposed a solution, and any of them could have done the job. In cases where multiple options could suffice, your opportunity to win the sale is more likely to come from the manner in which your product is being positioned to the customer, rather than from the solution itself. That's where valuable intangible qualities like the salesperson's credibility, integrity, knowledge, strategic vision, and advice become important tie breakers.

What is the value of working with a knowledgeable and trustworthy salesperson instead of a vendor whose methods are somewhat questionable? The difference can be huge from the customer's perspective, even if the products being offered are virtually identical. In sales, the customer's perception of your value is equal to the benefits of your product or service plus the intangibles you bring to the table.

> "In sales, the customer's perception of your value is equal to the benefits of your product or service plus the intangibles you bring to the table."

From my point of view, it's no longer enough to be friendly and polite. There are plenty of salespeople in the world who are nice. The concept of selling yourself is more about accruing enough value to tip the scales in your favor, whether you are up against a competitive proposal, or you are competing against the decision to do nothing. We also want to accumulate enough value to overcome any concerns that may arise when dealing with objections.

Whether salespeople are born with character traits like credibility, integrity, knowledge, helpfulness, candor, or respect, is debatable. What we are really talking about is the skill of being able to convey these intangibles throughout the sales process, so sellers who think strategically and use these skills can be perceived as more valuable resources than their competitors. That's where your overall sales strategy along with specific QBS techniques become very important. As I said before, even if you are the most valuable salesperson in your industry, you still must say and do things that will cause you to be perceived as such.

How to Gain Instant Credibility

Salespeople are always looking to put their best foot forward. As a result, the tendency among sellers is to look for opportunities to point out all of the valuable features of their products and services. Some people reading this book might think, "I don't do that." Again, maybe you don't. But, during your last job interview when the hiring manager said, "Tell me about yourself," did you respond with a lengthy account of your background as evidence that you would be a good employee?

The natural inclination to highlight certain selling points may be rooted in good intentions, but focusing on yourself or your products doesn't necessarily speak to the customer's needs or their specific buying motivations. Let me give you a real life example of how doing the exact opposite can instantly change the perception of your customer.

Back in the mid-1980's, I got tired of paying monthly rent for a two bedroom apartment, so one day, I pulled into the

Merrill Lynch Realty office on my way home from work. Because it was early evening, there were only a few cars left in the parking lot. I walked into the lobby and stood in front of an empty reception desk for a few moments until I noticed the customer service bell on the counter.

"Ding...ding!," I rang the bell for service.

A well-dressed gentleman suddenly appeared in the doorway, saying, "Can I help you?"

"My name is Tom Freese," I said. "I am tired of paying rent to an apartment complex. And, since I pass your office building every day on my way home from work, I wanted to stop in and find out what it would take to buy a house."

"I'm Jerry Saunders," the man said, greeting me with an outstretched hand. "Come on back to my desk and we'll take a look."

We sat down in his cubicle area and I explained my situation. At the time, I was not married but had a decent job, and, with the exception of paying off my student loan, I had no debt to speak of. Jerry inquired what type of house I wanted, but honestly, I hadn't even gotten that far yet in my thought process.

To get the ball rolling, Jerry suggested that we set aside an afternoon or two to ride around and look at homes, so I could can get a sense for what was on the market.

The following Tuesday, I arrived back at the Merrill Lynch office promptly at three o'clock. Jerry was waiting for me with a stack of MLS listings he had printed out prior to my arrival. At the time, only licensed agents could print "specs-pages" for properties registered with the Multiple Listing Service.

"Why don't you pick a dozen or so listings that look interesting to you," Jerry said, "and then we'll hit the road." I did, and we were off.

On the way to the first listing, we exchanged pleasantries while cruising along in Jerry's brand new Cadillac Deville. When we arrived at the first house, Jerry got the key out of the lockbox and opened the front door. As soon as I stepped foot into the house, I remember having an emotional moment—thinking, "This house could some day be mine." I was about to purchase my very first home. Momma's boy was growing up!

A voice from over my shoulder snapped me out of my short-lived daydream. "You don't want this house," Jerry said dismissively. A bit surprised, I turned around to hear the rest of the story.

"Tom, see this crack in the tile," he said pointing to the foyer floor. "If you look closely, the crack goes up the wall and then across the ceiling. I think this house has a structural problem," he said. Jerry suggested that we look around anyway to see what ideas we could glean from the floor plan and design features. Sure enough, when we went down into the basement, there was a three-quarter inch crack in the foundation. Jerry was right, I didn't want this house.

What do you supposed happened to Jerry's credibility at that moment? As an advisor, his value to me instantly skyrocketed. It was suddenly very apparent that this guy wasn't just trying to sell me a house. Instead, he seemed to be acting as my advocate. Like Toto in the *The Wizard of Oz*, he was basically pulling back the curtain in an effort to help me buy the right house.

By the time we walked through the front door of the third listing, my confidence as a potential buyer had increased significantly. "I don't want this house," I announced to Jerry.

"Why not?" he asked.

I pointed to the shag carpet which was three or four shades more obnoxious than Pepto-Bismol pink. Combined with the peach colored walls and light blue trim, the place looked utterly dreadful.

"Uggg-ly," Jerry agreed. But, as the voice of experience, Jerry pointed out that the carpet in any of these "starter" homes would need to be replaced and the walls would probably get a fresh coat of paint. "If you can look beyond the carpet and paint color," he suggested, "you should focus on finding a house that is structurally sound and has a desirable floor plan. Those are things that are not easily changed."

We looked at several more houses that day and more the following week. Guess which house I ended up buying? Yep, the one with the pink carpets. With a fresh coat of neutral colored paint on the walls and newly installed carpeting, the house looked great—completely different from what I originally saw when it was on the market.

Honestly, the idea of looking for houses while being flanked by an over-eager real estate agent trying to "sell" me on the benefits of each listing would have been nauseating, to say the least. Like most buyers, I didn't want to be "sold to," especially not by a commission hungry real estate salesperson. What I wanted (and needed) was someone I could trust, not only to provide insight about what to look for, but also to help me know what to avoid when buying a home. I have since bought four homes from Jerry Saunders, now of ReMax North Atlanta, as the result of him solidifying his credibility in my eyes as a competent and candid real estate professional.

Help Customers Make Smart Decisions

The temptation for sellers to always be "selling," meaning putting their best foot forward to try and impress potential buyers, is very strong. Rather than just promoting the wonderful benefits that will come from purchasing your product or service, sellers must learn to think about conveying value from the customer's perspective. The specific benefits you provide are only wonderful and valuable to the extent that customers recognize the need that's being addressed.

Take the product I sell, for example—sales training. The value proposition of my company, QBS Research, Inc., is highly intangible. Although Question Based Selling is well documented in books and in the training curriculums we deliver, you can't actually touch the QBS Methodology, or hold specific sales strategies in your hand. Therefore, the only way for us to create business opportunities is to somehow cause decision makers at potential client accounts to perceive large amounts of value when they discuss or evaluate our programs.

I've noticed over the years, however, that sales managers and executives are much more interested in knowing how QBS will address their problems (P), than hearing all the wonderful things about our training solutions (S). Whether the client is trying to bring more deals into the pipeline, create differentiation, protect profit margins, ramp up new salespeople, better qualify forecasted accounts, or close more deals, the need to accomplish each of these goals is what creates a sense of urgency to move forward with QBS.

If we agree that customers are more interested in addressing their own problems, issues, and concerns than they are in hearing a generic sales pitch, then it stands to reason that your value proposition should revolve around the customer's issues, as seen from their point of view. As a result, I focus most of my energy talking with potential client managers, executives, and salespeople about the challenges posed by the current selling environment and economic conditions, rather than just rattling off a litany of our courseware's benefits. For example, this is how I might position QBS to a potential client. I would explain:

Freese: *"Question Based Selling is very different from traditional methods. Most of the sales training that's currently being offered is process training, which is fine. But, just defining the steps of the sales process is no longer a differentiator for most sales organizations. Your competitors have a sales process in place, too, and their process is probably very similar to yours.*

Just defining the sales process isn't the problem most organizations face anyway. You don't need to hire me to come in and tell your salespeople that Step 1 is: Identify New Opportunities, Step 2 is: Uncovering Needs, and so on. The problem sellers face on a daily basis isn't knowing "what" to do, it's figuring out "how" to execute more effectively on those objectives, to produce a higher return on invested effort.

As you know, today's competitive selling environment has changed dramatically over the last several months, if not years. Potential buyers are more cautious and standoffish than ever before. As a result, customers with less time are being targeted by more salespeople, and

*they no longer have the patience or inclination to spend
time with every salesperson who comes calling..."*

First and foremost, customers want to know that you understand their problems, issues, and concerns. This doesn't happen
by spewing out a bunch of product features and benefits. Do
you remember the PAS positioning discussion from Chapter 3?
What I'm really doing in the sample dialogue above is pulling
back the curtains and pointing at the metaphoric 'crack on the
foyer tile,' identifying issues that may not be so obvious to
people who are struggling to make decisions.

During my conference calls with potential clients, I am
happy to explain the different QBS training options, as well as
how much they cost. But, our value proposition must be
explained against the backdrop of a realistic discussion that
starts with the competitive challenges sales organizations
currently face, and why continuing with a traditional approach
may no longer be a viable alternative. If you want to sell yourself, you must successfully demonstrate that you understand the
customer's goals, interests, and concerns—just like we talked
about doing in a job interview scenario.

The moment a potential client starts to form the impression
that, "Hey, this guy understands my situation and I think he can
help us!", is when you begin to gain serious traction in the
conversation and establish your credibility as a valuable resource.

Here's the cool part. Once you have demonstrated that you
do understand the customer's challenges, your company's value
proposition can basically be summed up in a few words, by
saying, "Those are exactly the issues we help clients solve." The
next thing the customer will ask is, "How do you do that?"

Doesn't that sound like a *mini-invitation?* Talking with people about the problems they face is also one of the easiest ways to pique their interest. Predictably, interested customers will want to find out more about how you might be able to help them address their challenges. From there, it's easy to suggest a face-to-face meeting, a conference call, or some other appropriate next step. Either way, the net result of taking

> "Talking with people about the problems they face is also one of the easiest ways to pique their interest."

a PAS approach is so very different from what would have happened had I gone down the typical path of glorifying all the wonderful benefits of Question Based Selling.

This same principle applies to virtually any type of intangible sale. Take financial services, for example. With the rollercoaster ride people experienced in the 1990's, and then again just recently, customers have developed a fair amount of skepticism toward brokers, agents, bankers, and financial advisors. Nowadays, if you are a financial advisor calling prospective clients, jumping head first into a diatribe about your successful track record probably isn't going to be enough to earn the customer's trust. A better way to demonstrate your knowledge of the industry and bond with prospective clients in the process might be to point at some of the proverbial 'cracks in the tile,' just like Jerry Saunders did. Go ahead and talk with people about some of the fundamental shifts that have occurred in the market and the challenges customers now face in terms of managing their investments.

Here are some other positioning statements from various value-based industries:

Financial Services:

"Mr. Customer, though our business is offering financial products and services, just giving recommendations to buy things and hoping for the best isn't good enough for clients anymore. Most of the people I deal with aren't wanting to hear the latest hot stock pick and they don't want to be pressured by a commission-hungry broker. Instead, clients want sound thinking and solid direction. They want an integrity-based financial partner who will help maximize their return on investment and manage risk. Customers also want someone who will invest the time to consider their specific financial situation, as well as long term investment objectives. Mr. Customer, that's basically what we do for the clients we serve."

Real Estate:

"Ms. Customer, I understand you are thinking about listing your home and are in the process of selecting an agent. The way I see it, most of the value homeowners get from working with a licensed realtor comes after the listing agreement is signed. In the current real estate market, selling a house is no longer as simple as taking a few photos of the home and then listing it with a friendly neighborhood broker. If you want to get quality offers on your property, your home must be proactively marketed—to other real estate agents and to the buying public. Leads have to be monitored and followed up on, and feedback should be used to deal with any issues that arise once the home is opened to prospective buyers. If you want results, you really need to choose an agent who will put forth the same effort they would when selling their own home ...which is precisely what we do!"

Medical:

"Dr. Smith, there are several medicines you can choose to prescribe for patients with chronic foot fungus. The problem is, most people aren't looking for a temporary solution. They want permanent relief. Consequently, the ultimate goal for these patients is for their doctor to prescribe a treatment plan that will not only eliminate the current itching, chafing, burning, and peeling, but will completely eradicate the underlying medical condition after a few weeks of consistent usage. That's exactly what this new product does."

Notice that the first thing the seller does in each of these scenarios is pull back the curtain and expose the reality customers are currently facing. What a novel idea—a salesperson who actually raises potential issues in order to help customers make good decisions!

You have to figure that decision makers are dealing with a number of challenges. Getting those issues to come up in your conversations with potential customers is always a challenge for sellers who are trying to break into new opportunities. This is where one hand literally washes the other. To be seen as a valuable resource, you must demonstrate that you understand and appreciate their current situation—problems, issues and concerns. Of course, when the issues you raise resonate with potential clients and you position yourself as a valuable resource, the perception that you can help them solve their problems will undoubtedly expand the conversation into a more in-depth discussion about the their objectives and your solutions.

What's the Cost of Not Buying?

Speaking of issues that are important to potential customers, the issue of price often tops the list. Talking with customers about price is not only acceptable, it's vital. We want customers to understand all the decision details (like cost) that will enable them to move forward with a purchase. In Chapter 4, when we talked about conversational dynamics, I even showed you how to redirect a customer's request for pricing into a more in-depth needs development conversation. At some point, however, the issue of cost will come back to the forefront and customers will have to decide whether the solution being proposed is worth the price.

If you are an experienced salesperson already, then you understand that cost justification is a critical part of every sale. Whether or not something is "worth the money," is totally subjective based solely on the customer's perception your recommended solutions plus with any additional value you personally bring to the table.

Customers will ask, "How much does it cost?" This is a valid question and you will no doubt provide all the relevant details for their consideration. But, in addition to just talking about pricing alternatives, the question that someone should really be asking is, "What's the cost of *not* buying the proposed product or service?" The answer to this question may actually prove to be the easiest way for customers to justify the value of a highly intangible purchase.

When we talked about the principles of *Being More Strategic with Your Sales Questions* in Chapter 5, I pointed out that the value of a proposed solution must exceed its cost for decision makers to pull the trigger on a purchase. This is true in every type of sales. But, that's not the whole story, especially if you sell big ticket items.

For example, suppose a salesperson tried to convince you that purchasing $100,000 in new computer equipment for your company would save $100,000 in ongoing maintenance costs. Would you consider that a good deal?

One could argue that since the amount saved covers the cost of the solution, this would be a sound business decision. Well, that's how the salesperson who submitted the bid might feel, but there's a logic problem with this from the customer's perspective. Asking a customer to pay a substantial sum for the promise of getting their money back, doesn't necessarily seem like a good deal to me. It probably won't seem like a good deal to them, either. Would you invest $100,000 of your own money in the hopes of getting a 0% return on that investment? I bet you wouldn't.

When clients who train their salespeople on QBS want to justify the expenditure, they're not just hoping to pay for the training. They wouldn't take their sales teams out of the field for two or three days unless they believed that the return on investment from the training would far exceed the cost. They expect to be paid back many times over.

I understand that customers have budgets and they have to be cautious and judicious with expenditures these days. But, what would happen if we thought outside the box for a moment, and asked: What's the cost of *not* doing a QBS training course? Well, if the cost of the training can easily be offset by signing one new account, QBS would no longer be an expense to the company. In fact, if you trained twenty-five or thirty reps on a sales team, and you realized an upside of one new account per person (per month), suddenly the QBS training becomes a money-maker, not a cost item. At that point, the cost of the actual training is insignificant compared to the cost of not doing it (in terms of lost opportunities).

Going back to the water pump metaphor, for a moment, how much does it cost to pump water out of a flooded basement? I suppose that would depend on the cost of the pump and the size of your basement. But, consider for a moment the opposite question. What's the cost of not getting the water out of the basement in a timely manner? That's a whole different story. Now, all kinds of issues are being brought into play, like the possibility of further structural damage, damage to personal property, mold or mildew, damage to furnace or electrical systems, potential health hazard, safety, infestation, displacement of the family, irreplaceable heirlooms, stress, insurance, clean up, time/hassle, resale value, and odor issues.

What's the likelihood that customers will consider every one of these implications in their cost analysis? Slim. They might focus on one or two implications, possibly three or four, but not all. So, I ask, who's going to bring up the rest? If not you, then you're leaving the door wide open for a competitor to be seen as a more valuable resource, and also to be in a stronger position to justify their solutions.

Think about this. Given the recent turbulence in the economy, what's the cost of not having a good financial advisor? Besides potentially missing out on positive upward runs when the market is showing strength, you could also incur unnecessary downside risk if the financial markets take another hit.

What's the cost of not having the appropriate amount of life insurance in the event of an untimely death? The answer to that will partly depend on the person. A billionaire probably doesn't need to think about life insurance. For the rest of us, what's the cost of your family not being able to count on your income, or the longer term cost of your kids not being able to go to college?

In terms of justifying a purchase decision, it's impossible to calculate the exact cost of not buying a product or service. The calculation itself would be totally subjective, based on many intangible implications that cannot be measured empirically. But, that does not mean those costs aren't real. For example, what's the cost of having a mildew problem in your home caused by excessive moisture? Who knows how to calculate that, but the desire to avoid the problem can provide significant motivation for homeowners to purchase a water pump. The same is true with regard to estimating the cost of your kids not going to college. It may not even be feasible to try and approximate these costs in actual dollars. But, I can tell you that the long term security of my own family was the primary justification that caused me to purchase my first life insurance policy with Northwestern Mutual Life in July, 1994.

Translation is the Key

Hopefully, some of the pieces of the puzzle are starting to fit together. Knowing that most customers aren't going to fully articulate their needs, one of the greatest ways a seller can provide value, and cause customers to perceive substantially more value, is to help them identify issues and needs they wouldn't necessarily have recognized on their own.

Earlier, I suggested that you should arm yourself with a repository of potential issues and implications that could potentially impact the customer's decision. Each time you identify another facet of the customer's need that can be addressed by your solution, you make it easier for customers to cost justify a purchase. Hence, creating multiple reasons for customers to want to buy from you is one of the easiest ways to create separation between yourself and competitive offerings. If a decision maker has nine or ten reasons to purchase your product, but only two reasons to go with a competitor, you will be in a much stronger position to win the business.

Translating the capabilities of your solutions into perceived value for the customer will always be one of the keys to being successful in a competitive selling environment.

Gold Medals & German Shepherds

Since we're talking about how to motivate potential customers to pull the trigger on a purchase, let's spend a moment revisiting the concept of *Gold Medals* and *German Shepherds.*

When I first developed Question Based Selling, it was clear to me that decision makers in most industries have a wide range of priorities, perspectives, and personal hot buttons that ultimately impact their buying preferences. However, at the end of the day, customers are motivated in essentially two ways—by positive reward and negative aversion. Hence, I created a metaphor in my first book (*Secrets of Question Based Selling*), to suggest that while some people are motivated to run fast toward *Gold Medals,* many others run even faster from *German Shepherds.*

Does your product offer positive benefits like high performance, cost effectiveness, enhanced customer satisfaction, or increased productivity? Benefits like these will often register a great deal of value with customers who are motivated by positive rewards (*Gold Medal* benefits). But, somewhere in your company's value proposition, I bet you also protect customers against certain downside risks, like protecting the data on your computer, exceeding your budget, or having dissatisfied customers. This ability to protect against or prevent problems also represents real value to customers, especially for those customers who are motivated by *German Shepherds*.

Positioning positive benefits to *Gold Medal* buyers is a great way to accrue value, but positioning the *German Shepherd* aspects of your product or service can be just as valuable. Because the vast majority of customers are motivated by a combination of *Gold Medal* and *German Shepherd* benefits, I recommend that you make a point to always position your proposed solutions both ways. Doing so does not change your product or the customer's requirements. The only thing that changes when you position the *Gold Medal* and *German Shepherd* aspects of your offering is the customer's perception of your value—it doubles!

This technique isn't new to marketers and advertisers. If you look closely, this strategy is already being used with everyday products. For example, why do people choose Johnson's Baby Shampoo? While some people buy it because it is gentle on the hair (*Gold Medal*), other people like the product because it won't sting their baby's eyes (*German Shepherd*). Remember the familiar slogan, "no more tears?" Frankly, both the positive and the negative justifications are valuable, as customers buy Johnson's Baby Shampoo because it is gentle on the hair *and* also because it won't sting their baby's eyes.

Why do people buy Volvo automobiles? Some people like Volvo because they manufacture elegant and stylish, luxury automobiles. Other people feel Volvo stands for safety, and protecting themselves and their family in the event of an automobile accident is very important. Once again we have the best of both worlds, where maximum value is registered when customers perceive both *Gold Medal* and *German Shepherd* benefits.

Note that it's natural for sellers to gravitate more toward one or the other, either the positive aspects of their product or the negative ones, based on their own personal preferences and inclinations. Rather than focusing on whatever motivates *us*, however, we must remember that the goal here is causing customers to recognize maximum value. Thus, the best way to maximize your probability of success for winning the business, and also for having very satisfied customers, is to always position in terms of *Gold Medals* and *German Shepherds*.

Cost Justification: The Final Hurdle

Cost justifying the decision is generally the final hurdle that must be cleared before customers are willing to pull the trigger on a purchase. When selling to individuals, cost justification might be as simple as buyers weighing the different options in their head before making a decision on the spot. In the corporate environment, a detailed cost analysis can sometimes drag on for weeks and involve multiple levels of authority and all kinds of political wrangling. Either way, the perceived value of your solution must justify the cost.

Let me give you a little known secret about cost justification—depth of conversation is a salesperson's best friend. As we discussed earlier, people don't just buy umbrellas in case it rains, or even to avoid getting wet. People buy umbrellas because of the underlying implications—wanting to preserve a professional image, be comfortable, protect their clothes, avoid catching a cold, and to limit exposure to ultraviolet rays.

Can you differentiate the *Gold Medal* benefits on this list from the *German Shepherds*? Whatever value is perceived from each point accumulates into a total sense of worth, that again, cannot be measured empirically. While a customer might be able to calculate the cost of a leather jacket damaged by the rain, there is no way to calculate exactly what it's worth for someone to avoid getting sick, or the value of a business person looking and feeling their best when they show up for an important meeting.

Therefore, it's debatable whether one can ever calculate the true value of any product or service. I say you can't. You can esti-mate a value. The problem is, if you ask five different people to calculate the exact value of something that depends on a person's perspective, you would receive five different amounts. Valuation at that point is based on the person's perception, which is highly subjective. In sales we see this all the time. Someone who likes a particular product or service can make it look good on paper, while someone else in the same account who doesn't like the solution, will almost certainly calculate a value that is signifi-cantly lower. For buyers, it's a simple matter of perspective. Different strokes for different folks, as they say.

For sellers, cost justification is more about expanding the buyer's perspective. Since buyers tend to focus on a few specific hot buttons (usually whatever has their immediate attention), you can accumulate more value by getting customers to broaden their perception and recognize needs or appreciate facets of your solution that would otherwise go unnoticed.

That's where your newfound needs development skills come in. If you have done your homework and constructed a repository of issues and implications, there might easily be ten or more implications relating to any issue that could impact your customers. If you asked me to coach you as I listened in on one of your actual sales calls, I would make a series of tiny tick marks every time I heard the customer say something like, "Good point," or, "That's right," or, "Yes, that's important, too." Every time it was clear that you raised an important issue or implication that took the conversation into more depth, I would make a tiny tick mark on my notepad. Once you learned what to listen for, you would begin to do the same on subsequent calls. If you are consciously accumulating value points in your mind, chances are good that you are accumulating value with your customer as well.

> "If you are consciously accumulating value points in your mind, chances are good that you are accumulating value with your customer as well."

How do you empirically measure the credibility of a salesperson in the eyes of their customers? The answer is, you can't. Still, teaching salespeople how to establish more credibility sooner can have a tremendous positive impact on the effectiveness and productivity of an entire sales organization. Similarly, you can't empirically measure competitive differentiation. But if you can show sellers how to differentiate themselves in a competitive marketplace, these subtle but very important intangibles might be the difference between earning the customer's confidence, or sounding the same as everyone else.

By the way, what's the cost of not differentiating yourself in a job interview or on a sales call? It turns out that some of your most valuable attributes don't actually show up as line items on your resume, nor are they listed in your company's product brochure. Qualities like integrity, desire, vision, creativity, confidence, poise, honesty, compassion, resourcefulness, and work ethic tend to be very important to people who are forming impressions about you and the value you offer. Even though you can't actually touch these things, your ability to demonstrate and convey valuable character traits will not only determine whether you succeed in selling yourself, but also reflect how much others are willing to pay for your services.

Chapter 8

Making Prospects More Receptive to Your Message

Sellers should have a compelling story to tell about their products and services, but you must also have a receptive audience who wants to hear about your potential solutions. Particularly since today's buyer is increasingly cautious, decision makers are quick to fend off even the most tenacious salespeople.

Rather than being more aggressive, however, why not take the opposite approach? To engage more people in more productive conversations about their needs and your value, let's use sound logic and good technique to first pique their curiosity.

The days of trying to smooth-talk prospective customers into buying a product or service are over. Most customers don't want to be "smooth-talked," and they are no longer willing to be pushed, pressured, or persuaded by a commission-hungry salesperson who is personally motivated to close deals by the end of the month. I'm not trying to indict our beloved profession, but the traditional approach to dealing with customers probably does need to be injected with a dose of reality for what makes sense in the current business environment.

The typical buyer's standoffishness toward salespeople and their defense mechanisms are definitely on the rise, but this trend isn't necessarily new. Decision makers have been skeptics of the proverbial product pitch for a long time. But, the sheer increase in the volume of sales calls that customers now receive has done a lot to change their receptiveness toward sellers.

In the old days, when salespeople literally had to show up in person to call on a customer, decision makers dealt with far fewer vendors under arguably less sophisticated business conditions. The recent explosion in technology and the shift to tele-sales and other media related access means customers are now being deluged by sales callers, who are all vying for a precious slice of the customer's time and attention, and ultimately, a share of their budget dollars.

Up to now, the usual strategy for dealing with standoffish customers has been for sellers to simply be more aggressive in their attempts to penetrate accounts and overcome the customer's defenses. Many salespeople still believe that using forceful tactics is the only way to be taken seriously. Maybe you're familiar with the movie, *Glengarry Glen Ross*, where Alec Baldwin plays the role an obnoxious sales manager who declares that, "Selling is a simple matter of ABC: "Always be closing!"

This kind of thinking has actually created a predictable backlash over time. Persistent hounding on the part of sales-people has caused customers to be even more cautious and reserved. Meanwhile, this increased resistance on the part of prospective customers has ironically caused sellers to be even more aggressive. A crazy kind of cycle.

Let's review what we know. We know that decision makers

tend to buy from people they feel comfortable with and trust. That's why it's so important to be seen as a trusted advisor within your accounts. We also know that establishing credibility and building relationships with potential customers is the key to understanding the customer's needs and earning the right to recommend potential solutions. As a salesperson, it's easy to set your sights on the goal of making a sale. The problem is, how do you forge relationships with someone who is holding you off at arm's length? Furthermore, how is a salesperson in today's competitive marketplace supposed to get past the customer's initial defenses to engage them in a productive dialogue?

Piquing the interest of skeptical prospects is the first hump to get over in the sales process, and arguably one of the biggest challenges sellers face. It's also one of the least talked about subjects in sales training over the last thirty years. That's because the skill set

> "Piquing the interest of skeptical prospects is the first hump to get over in the sales process, and arguably one of the biggest challenges sellers face."

required for sellers to transform customers from being cautious and standoffish into wanting to engage is not very well understood. Building relationships with key decision makers in target accounts is understandably tough, particularly since lots of other sellers are vying for the same customer's time and attention.

Having the ability to always say the right thing at the right time is a special gift. If you happen to be one of those natural conversationalists, it's certainly easier to strike up a dialogue with prospective customers. Most of us, however, fear the awkwardness and traditional risks of rejection that come with reaching out to potential buyers. We understand that decision makers aren't just sitting next to the telephone waiting for another salesperson to call. And, when the phone does ring, we know from experience that most buyers default to holding salespeople at arms length. Heck, that's why they call it *cold-calling*.

Until now, salespeople have been taught that selling is simply a numbers game, and that the inherent risk of rejection is just part of the job. Contact as many leads as possible in the hopes of identifying some subset of potential customers, then whittle that group down into a smaller collection of bona fide prospects. Some fraction of those prospects will become qualified opportunities, and some subset of those will hopefully turn into deals. The prevailing thought in this game has always been, to increase sales, you simply had to make more calls.

This notion of funneling your leads down into a smaller subset of suspects, prospects, qualified opportunities, and then closed sales, is still valid. But, rather than burning through tons of possibilities just to net out a few desirable deals, the focus has shifted from just making lots of sales calls to actually increasing the effectiveness and productivity of each call.

The study of sales effectiveness was the original catalyst that created the QBS Methodology, as our focus has always been on increasing a salesperson's return on invested sales effort. Simply put, if it was possible to adjust your approach in a way that would make customers more receptive to your messages, and ultimately boost your sales, would you be open to the possibility of doing something different? If so, there is one particular ingredient in the success formula for selling yourself that you should pay particular attention to from this day forward. Allow me to set the stage.

My grandmother (Nana, we called her) always made the best brownies in town. These delectable delights would literally melt in your mouth. Anybody can whip up a batch of brownies, but there was definitely something special about Nana's brownies that raised them head and shoulders above all others. Of course, I can't tell you the exact ingredients because that's a closely guarded family secret. However, I can share a different secret with you—the secret to *making customers more receptive*, in order to raise yourself head and shoulders above other sales reps.

The secret ingredient is *curiosity*. It's a simple formula really. If a decision maker is not the least bit curious about who you are or what you can do for him, then you probably won't succeed in getting his or her time or attention. Fortunately for the strategic salesperson, the opposite is also true. If you are able to do something that piques the prospect's curiosity, you will not only get more mindshare within target accounts, you will also enjoy a competitive advantage throughout the sales process.

Curiosity: The Genesis of Every Sale

Because I was a salesperson before becoming a trainer, my focus when delivering QBS Methodology courses (or when writing books) has always been on the implementation of the material, not just the transfer of information. What you learn in a seminar or by reading a book is only valuable if you can apply it in the real world. Of course, when something you try works really well, the goal then is to understand why it worked so you can repeat your success in future customer situations.

The QBS Methodology was designed to be a recipe for

repeatable success. Rather than expecting each salesperson in the organization to re-invent the wheel through their individual trials and tribulations, what if we provided an easy to follow blueprint that could also be duplicated across the group? My goal isn't to transform your sales team into a bunch of script readers. But, to the extent that the larger sale is generally an accumulation of smaller successes throughout the sales process, we should be able to identify the ingredients necessary to implement an effective step-by-step formula. In Question Based Selling, we call this formula the *Conversational Layering Model.*

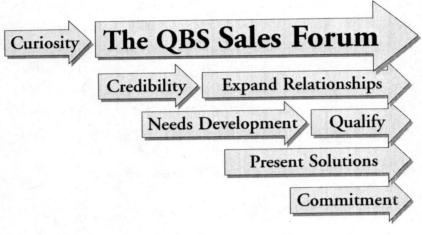

(Figure 8.1)

The above diagram represents the logical flow of a sales conversation, starting in the upper left and cascading downward toward the lower right. Each of the arrows in the graphic represents an important element on the way to achieving the larger goal of making a sale. Following the direction of the arrows gives us a roadmap identifying each of the prerequisites necessary to transition to the next appropriate step in the sales process. If you are able to identify and execute each of the steps in this logical progression, your likelihood of making a sale is significantly enhanced. The best way to understand how Conversational Layering works is for me to explain it in reverse, working backwards from the desired end result.

Ultimately, the goal of every salesperson is to secure commitments from qualified customers (lower right of diagram). We want decision makers to choose to partner with us over other competitive options, and we want them to recognize enough value to move forward with a purchase of our recommended products and services.

Working backward in the diagram, in order to secure this level of commitment from potential buyers, you must present valuable solutions. Very few prospects will commit without having a sense of how they might benefit from your product or service. Working backwards once again, before you can present a valuable solution, you must first identify a need—a problem, issue, goal, or objective. It's impossible to provide value without the existence of a need. Qualification is another part of the discovery process, which is why it's on the same level as needs development. Mutually beneficial business transactions should be good for both the customer and vendor. Can you follow the logical progression of the prerequisite steps needed to achieve the broader objective in the sales process?

Unfortunately, this is where the logic ends in traditional sales models, as 'probing' for needs often marks the beginning of the traditional sales process. Remember, you can ask whatever questions you want once a customer sees you as a valuable resource and wants to share information with you. But if you are forging new relationships, you should expect to encounter a certain level of standoffishness as prospective customers in the real world are reluctant to share information with just anyone who calls.

So, here's the million dollar question. How is a salesperson supposed to engage potential customers in a conversation about their needs when they default to being standoffish toward salespeople? The answer can be found in the upper left of the *Conversational Layering* diagram (Figure 8.1). The two most important ingredients for engaging prospects in productive conversation are *Curiosity* and *Credibility*, both of which are enablers for the rest of the sales process.

We already talked about establishing credibility (Chapter 6) by kicking off your needs development conversations with a series of short answer, *diagnostic questions*. When forging new relationships, sellers can earn a lot more credibility by asking strategic questions than by making claims about their products. But, before you start barraging customers with questions, you must first secure the customer's time and attention. In QBS, we say you have to have a *Forum* for selling.

How do you secure a prospect's time and attention in today's competitive marketplace when they are accustomed to fending salespeople off on a daily basis? That's where our secret ingredient comes into play—leveraging *curiosity* in the sales process.

I would argue that curiosity is the genesis of every sale. I'll say it again. If a prospect or customer is not the least bit curious about who you are or what you can do for them, then you probably won't succeed in getting their time or their attention. Fortunately the opposite is true. As prospects and customers become more curious about what you or your products can do for them, you get more mindshare in target accounts.

So, let me ask, what are you doing to leverage curiosity as part of your strategic sales process?

Don't be alarmed if you haven't spent much time thinking about leveraging curiosity in your sales before now. You can go to your local bookstore and pour through every business book on the shelf, and notwithstanding my work, the topic of curiosity is essentially untouched. Isn't that strange—sales drives every company, and curiosity drives every sale, but we're not even talking about how to leverage it?!

Creating Sparks of Interest

Just making people curious is not the goal in Question Based Selling. What we really want is to engage potential buyers in a productive conversation about their needs, in a way that enables us to establish credibility, build relationships, convey the value of our solutions, and ultimately, secure a commitment to move forward with a sales transaction. Making them interested, or piquing the customer's curiosity, simply becomes the means to accomplishing these goals.

> "Curiosity is the spark that causes people to want to know more."

Curiosity is actually a very powerful human emotion. It's the spark that causes people to want to know more. Whenever someone becomes curious about something, they tend to focus all of their attention on that, and everything else fades to the background. This is particularly good for salespeople, since one of our primary functions is to grab the attention of key decision makers in targeted prospect accounts.

If you are on board with the idea that curiosity provides the spark that ignites the rest of the sales process, let's talk more specifically about how to induce curiosity, and how to incorporate this strategy into your daily interactions with prospective and existing customers. Ironically, some of the techniques we've already talked about are also some of the most valuable for piquing the prospect's interest.

Mini-Invitations are HUGE!

Mini-invitations are terrific conversational tools, as we discussed earlier in Chapter 4. They are also great curiosity inducers. In an account where you have an existing relationship and the customer is already open and willing to share with you, you may not need a curiosity strategy. But, if your job function includes business development, and you are responsible for creating revenue opportunities that otherwise wouldn't exist, then using mini-invitations to make your audience more receptive can pay huge dividends.

Basically, a mini-invitation is the customer's way of saying, "Tell me more." It's the equivalent of a decision maker saying, "Mr. Salesperson, I'm interested enough to keep going with this, so could you please take a few minutes and explain your solutions?" Of course, their interest (in the form of an invitation) paves the way for you to educate them. Similarly, if a customer said, "Ms. Salesperson, could you please ask me a couple specifics to better understand my needs?", that would instantly change the complexion and receptiveness of your sales interactions. Customers would shift from being naturally standoffish to being intrigued, to the point where they will actually invite you to lead the conversation. Look again at the words from one of the examples I referenced earlier.

Salesperson: *"Hi, Ms. Jones, my name is Bart Burton with Integrated Printing Supplies here in Little Rock. We realize that you may have a source for office equipment already, which is perfectly fine. We specialize in print supplies. But, the value we offer customers is unique, because we basically solve the problems that traditional toner vendors have created, and save customers money in the process."*

Office Mgr: *"What problems do you solve?"*

Bingo! When a customer asks for more information, they instantly become much more receptive to what you have to say. This technique doesn't guarantee that you always will make a sale, but I can pretty much guarantee you won't sell anything if you aren't able to pique the customer's interest.

Look at the meaning of the words. The customer here is essentially saying, "Can you please take a few minutes and explain how you can be a valuable resource to us?" That's a nice invitation from a curious prospect, don't you think?

This type of positioning works in every industry. While one could argue that some of this is just common courtesy, using curiosity to create mini-invitations is highly strategic because it generates such predictable outcomes. A salesperson in the financial services industry, for example, could say, "We solve many of the problems that traditional investment vehicles have created for investors." Unless someone was dead set against talking to this person, the customer would be compelled to ask, "What problems do you solve?" Just like that, this customer has suddenly become more receptive.

A medical supplies rep selling therapeutic devices could easily say to a doctor or clinician, "This device was designed to solve some of the issues that traditional treatment protocols have created." And so on, and so on. This method of engaging potential buyers is repeatable because the problem solving theme is ultimately what your value proposition is built around anyway.

Curiosity Facilitates Needs Development

I mentioned earlier that my first needs development question is almost always the same. At the point when it's appropriate to inquire about the customer's needs, I say, *"Can I ask you a couple specifics about _____, so I can give you accurate information?"* Virtually everyone responds by saying, "Yes," or, "Sure." Besides just being invited to ask relevant questions, this is also a great way to induce curiosity. The underlying logic is simple. When someone invites you to ask questions, they also become curious about what you are going to ask.

Try this experiment. Strike up a conversation with someone at a dinner party or in the bleachers at your child's basketball game, and say to that person, "Can I ask you about something that I've been wondering about?" Then, watch the expression on their face. The other person will instantly lock in on you as if nothing else was happening in the world. You will have their complete attention, to the point where if they have just taken a bite of food, they will literally stop chewing. It's human nature—when someone becomes curious about something, they focus all of their attention on whatever they're curious about, and everything else fades to the background.

A word of caution: just because someone gives you permission to ask questions doesn't mean they will remain curious forever. This initial spark of interest must be followed with good technique (like *Diagnostic Questions*), allowing you to establish some initial credibility that will hopefully blossom and evolve into a longer-term business relationship.

Another way to create sparks of interest is to use the PAS positioning model we talked about in Chapter 3, as opposed to the traditional SPA approach. The typical elevator pitch is full of statements—as we discussed. Ironically, a litany of claims about a product or service usually does more to satisfy a prospect's curiosity than create it. Oops! On the other hand, facilitating a conversation about what's most important to the decision maker (their problems, issues, and concerns) does the exact opposite. Rather than satisfying the customer's curiosity with a self-serving rant about your value, every time a salesperson asks a relevant and intelligent question about the customer's need, you further pique their interest.

Let me show you what I mean when we play out the earlier dialogue.

Salesperson: *"Hi, Mr. Customer, Bart Burton with Integrated Printing Supplies located here in Little Rock. I realize that you may have a source for office equipment already, which is fine. We specialize in print supplies, but we also solve the problems that traditional toner vendors have created, and save customers* *money in the process."*

Customer: *"What problems do you solve?"*

Salesperson: *"Well, there are a number of tricks that get pulled in the toner business. Things like over-stocking supply shelves, substituting lesser quality products, or not keeping enough inventory and allowing customers to run out of product at the least opportune time. We are able to make these issues disappear because of how our service is set up. Would it make sense for me to give you a quick overview of how we do it?"*

At the end of the day, you bond with people on their problems, and your value proposition is only as great as the customer's perception of what they need. Customers who are curious and have lots of reasons to buy from you will have a greater sense of urgency to move forward. They will also have more interest in listening to your recommendations.

Piquing the Hiring Manager's Interest

As I've said, a formal job interview represents the ultimate sales situation. The interviewee is not only responsible for selling themselves, they are also the product being sold.

During the typical sales pitch (I mean job interview), most candidates respond to the question, "Can you tell me a little about yourself?", by doing just that—telling about themselves. They launch into a detailed description of their work history, education, experience, and family situation—in effect, they give their product pitch. The question I would ask is, does jumping into a litany about yourself do more to pique a hiring manager's interest or satisfy their curiosity?

The attributes you bring to the table and your personal goals and objectives might interest some employers. But, what's even more interesting and more important to most hiring managers are their own business and personal goals.

Whether you are competing for a position within your current company or looking for a new opportunity, you have a better chance of getting the nod if you have a distinct advantage over other candidates who are vying for the same position. If it's an attractive opportunity, you have to assume that the other candidates being considered also have a decent education, a reasonable work history, and a good looking resume, just like you. So, what's going to be your differentiator if the other candidates are comparable in capability, capacity, experience, knowledge, and personality? What will make you stand out?

Herein lies the value of piquing the customer's curiosity and using that same curiosity to cause decision makers to be more receptive to your message. If you can somehow pique the interest of potential customers (or hiring managers) in a way that causes them to become more curious about how you can help them or what you offer, this alone gives you a significant advantage.

One more time, let's revisit our sample interview verbiage.

Manager: *"Dale, thanks for meeting with me today. Can you tell me a little about yourself?"*

Candidate: *"Sure. Do you already have a copy of my resume?*

Manager: *"Yes, I have it right here."*

Candidate: *"Since you already have my work history, I would add that I am a hard working person with a decent track record. But, my guess is you may be looking for more than that to fill this position—perhaps some of the intangibles that don't always show up as specific line items on a resume.*

For example, I'm guessing that in addition to finding someone with knowledge and experience, you would want someone who could ramp up and become productive as quickly as possible. You might also be looking for someone who can blend well with the current culture, but who can also contribute new ideas and possibly a fresh perspective to the team. As long as we're hypothesizing, you may also be looking for someone with a positive attitude, who is self-motivated and extremely customer-focused. Am I close?"

Manager: *"Absolutely."*

Candidate: *"Well, those are the types of things that have enabled me to be successful in the past, and that's what I would bring to this position as well."*

The hiring manager's first impression is likely to be, "Wow, you sound very different than everyone else!" That's good because you want to be different! There's no question that raising issues that are important to the customer (or interviewer) will cause them to be more interested in whatever messages you are trying to convey. In fact, your ability to create these initial sparks of interest and cause customers to be more receptive to your potential value, may just be one of your biggest differentiators in the decision process.

Leveraging Curiosity with Voice-Mail and Email

Voice-mail has become an enemy for many sellers, and email is similarly losing ground as an effective prospecting tool. Isn't it strange how technological advances in communication have, in many cases, distanced salespeople from prospective buyers? That's because in our new electronic age, you're not the only one who's trying to leverage technology to penetrate new accounts.

The average call back rate when leaving a voice-mail has been reduced to between 2% to 5%, depending on your industry and what survey you happen to believe. That means there are tons of salespeople making calls and leaving voice-mail messages with prospects, but the vast majority of those calls are not being returned. Treating sales as a numbers game does very little to motivate a salesperson when their percentage chance of success is so astronomically low. Add to that the dismaying fact that if a prospective customer listens to your voice-mail and decides not to call you back, your chances of getting through next time are significantly reduced.

> "Treating sales as a numbers game does very little to motivate a salesperson when their percentage chance of success is so astronomically low.."

What if it was possible to reverse this trend? Seriously, if you were able to leave voice-mail messages that caused 70% to 80% of the recipients to promptly return your calls, wouldn't voice-mail suddenly become a valuable sales asset, rather than a liability? How about a similar turnaround in results with email? This reversal can absolutely happen if you are open to changing your messaging strategy.

Let me boil this down to make it easy. There are only two possible motivators that cause people to respond to voice-mail messages. One thing that causes people to return calls is obligation. If the president of your company calls and leaves you a voice-mail message, you will return that call, probably sooner rather than later. Likewise, if an important customer calls and leaves a message, you will surely call them back. If your mother leaves a message on your voice-mail, you should call her back— she's your mom! But, what percent of prospects feel similarly obligated to return cold calls from salespeople? In that context, is anyone surprised the average call back rate is low?

The only other thing that causes people to respond to voice-mail messages is *curiosity*. Let me say it one more time. If someone is not the least bit interested in who you are or what you can do for them, then they are not going to return your call. Fortunately, the opposite is true. If you are able to induce curiosity with the voice-mail messages you leave, your probability of getting a return call increases dramatically.

I am not a fan of sales tricks, so I can tell you there's no place for gimmicks or clever one-liners when leaving curiosity-inducing voice-mail messages. Getting a high call-back rate when leaving voice-mail messages (or sending emails) is more about technique than gimmickry. If I left five different voice-mail messages with five different prospects, I might leave five completely different messages. My strategy for inducing curiosity would be consistent, but the script would change slightly based on the customer's scenario.

The biggest mistake sellers make with voice-mail is sounding just like everyone else. That's the quickest way to commoditize your value, or in the case of voice-mail, commoditize your reason for calling. The second biggest mistake sellers make is leaving a voice-mail message that actually satisfies the recipient's curiosity, which is exactly the opposite of our objective. Oops again!

Here's a typical voice-mail message from a vendor:

Voice-mail: *"Good afternoon, my name is Joe Smith and I'm with XYZ Company, the leading provider of widgets in North America. We offer valuable solutions for companies like yours and I wanted to see if there might be an opportunity to benefit you as well. If you get a minute, I would love to talk with you. I can be reached at (770) 123-4567. Have a great day!"*

Blah, blah, blah...get in line! Most prospects won't return this call because the message sounds just like dozens of voice-mails they've already deleted from other vendors. They're not likely to feel obligated, and since it's just another cold call from an eager salesperson, they're certainly not going to be curious. Of course, they won't call back!

The alternative to sounding like everyone else is leaving a curiosity-inducing voice-mail message that actually piques the prospect's interest. How exactly can you do this? The key to success is being purposeful, relevant, and specific in the context of your message, as opposed to sounding generic. Let me show you a few samples. Say the words aloud as you read them.

Curiosity Inducing Voice-Mail Samples:

i.)   *"Hi, George, this is Pat Wilkins calling from The Dynamic Systems Group—I'm on the team that works with large industrial accounts in the Southeast. I was on a conference call with one of your counterparts last Wednesday afternoon just after lunch, and two issues came up that I thought might impact your platform decisions moving forward, one of which is time sensitive. I wanted to be proactive and try to catch you in the office this afternoon. If you get a chance today, could you please call me back at (770) 123-4567?"*

ii)   *"Hi, Dale, this is Lane Patterson with HJK Corporation. I'm on the team that supports healthcare accounts in Ohio. I was hoping to catch you for a minute because we've had 13 new announcements in the last three and a half months, two of which I believe will impact your patient statistics. If you get a chance today, could you please call me at (770) 123-4567?"*

(iii)   *"Hi, Steve, this is Joe Tomlin calling from Primary Partners. I manage a team that works with financial brokers in the tri-cities area. A file came across my desk yesterday morning that raised a flag regarding (insert something relevant) and I wanted to try and catch you in the office. If you get a chance today, could you please call me back at (770) 123-4567?"*

Please note that these are just sample voice-mail messages, and they are *not* intended to be copied and used as generic cold calling scripts. You don't want to leave scripted messages anyway, because anything that sounds generic will cause your calls to be perceived as purposeless. I merely pulled a few hypothetical scenarios out of the air as examples of possible curiosity-inducing voice-mails. But, the point should be made that the context of all the voice-mail messages I leave is intended to be purposeful and relevant, and the information referenced is always 100% accurate, or I wouldn't have said it.

My own call back rate, along with the success rates of students we teach, tends to be very high simply because purposeful and relevant voice-mail messages are curiosity-inducing. If the person who listens to your message wonders, "What two issues?", or, "a file came across your desk that raised a flag?", they will surely call you back. While there is an opportunity to recycle good ideas, it's critical that the context of your voice-mails are tailored to be congruent with whatever might be important to your target audience.

If we dig a little deeper, you may have noticed a few strategic nuances in the voice-mail samples above. For example, if you are initiating contact with new prospects, the first thing people want to know is who are you, and why are you calling? Just saying your name and company does not satisfy the need to know who you are. Are you the owner of the company, a customer service rep, or are you in some other role? Don't worry about having an impressive-sounding title. You just need to be relevant. Hence, it's easy to say, *"Hi, Dale, this is Lane Patterson with HJK Corporation, I'm on the team that supports healthcare accounts in Ohio."* Lane may or may not be a senior executive, but the fact that she's on the team that handles healthcare accounts in Ohio instantly makes her relevant to those accounts.

When you wrap up your voice-mail message, it's just as

important to have a forthright and clear request for action. I usually say, "*If you get a chance today, could you please call me back at (770) 123-4567.*" It's direct and to the point, but not overly forceful.

Sandwiched between the announcement of who you are and your request for action at the end of your voice-mail, is the gist of the message. The difference between the hundreds of generic voice-mail messages left by the masses and using a question-based approach is one word—curiosity. I try to leave voice-mail messages that not only grab the prospect's attention, but also spark a desire for them to call me back. Ultimately, I want people to feel compelled to return my calls.

When I deliver QBS training programs, people ask, "How exactly do you 'spark a desire' in people to get them to return calls?" It's a fair question and one that needs to be addressed in order to implement this technique and repeat your successes.

The first step is to understand the strategy behind the idea of leveraging curiosity. If your want to get return calls when you leave voice-mail messages, you must either depend on obligation or curiosity. Since very few customers feel obligated to return sales calls, leveraging curiosity is clearly the best option.

What is it exactly that makes people curious while listening to voice-mail messages? If you were sitting in my classroom, I would go do the board and draw a simple cause and effect diagram. 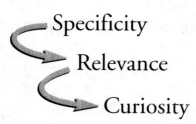 Specificity Relevance Curiosity

If the goal when leaving a voice mail is to induce curiosity, the intangible ingredient that creates curiosity is relevance. You cannot pique someone's curiosity by leaving irrelevant or generic voice-mail messages. How can you make your calls more relevant to potential customers? By working backward again, the magic when leaving effective voice-mail messages is specificity.

The main difference between my voice-mail messages and others is the fact that the ones I leave are intentionally specific. Did you notice how I mentioned there were two issues, one of which was "time sensitive?" In the second voice-mail, I referenced thirteen new announcements in the last three and a half months. Note that I didn't just say that we had "several new announcements," because that sounds generic. It's all about the details. I even went so far as to specifically indicate that the conference call last Wednesday occurred *just after lunch.*

Using specificity to create relevance (which breeds curiosity) is like adding seasoning to a steak before you throw it on the grill. Adding this level of specificity causes customers to form the impression that you're calling for a real reason and you know what you're talking about. If you say something that's relevant to them, of course they will want to expand the dialogue

This strategy of leveraging curiosity to increase your return call rate can be just as easily applied when reaching out to potential customers via email. I realize that people use email to accomplish a variety of different objectives. We all send, forward, and reply to lots of email messages during the course of a normal business day. Email has become a wonderful communication tool. But, if you want to use email as an effective prospecting device, you need to do something that will motivate potential customers to prioritize and respond to your email messages, and hopefully generate a live telephone conversation or a face-to-face meeting.

Once again, it's critical to recognize that you aren't the only salesperson using email to prospect. You can be sure that dozens of other vendors are targeting your same customers on a daily basis. As with voice-mail, most vendor email messages do more to satisfy a customer's curiosity than to induce it. You don't want to seem like a cold-caller on email any more than you would on the telephone. If your emails seem valueless to customers, they will do the same thing you and I do when we open Outlook and discover a lengthy list of e-offers featuring special discounts, limited time offers, and free shipping through the holidays. Delete, delete, delete.

If you want your email messages to be seriously considered and more importantly, responded to, then you'd better do something to pique the recipient's curiosity. How do you induce curiosity when sending emails?

Good news—the same logic we used for voice-mail applies to email. Specificity creates relevance, and relevance breeds curiosity. In other words, stop sending generic email messages! Even if your email makes it past the customer's corporate filter, generic emails are quickly discarded. Specificity also gives your emails purpose and credibility. Let me give you a quick example to illustrate. (see Figure 8.2)

Again, please don't just copy this message, and send it to your entire prospect data base. You can only expect a high response rate if the context of your emails is relevant to the intended recipient. That simply won't happen if you send out a bunch of generic emails.

Instead, pay more attention to the tone and theme of my sample email message. Notice that I am clearly contacting this customer for a reason—because two performance issues came up that I thought might impact her technology platform, one of

Subject: Per Joe Davis...

Kim,

My name is Jason Darden with XYZ Company and I'm on the team that works with manufacturing accounts in Northern California. I left you a quick voice-mail late last week and wanted to follow up this morning.

Last Wednesday, I talked with one of your managers in the Birmingham office and two performance issues came up that I think might impact your broader technology platform. One of those issues is time sensitive. I wanted to be proactive and see if it would make sense to brief you on the details.

Any chance we can set up a time to discuss later in the week? Please advise.

Jason

P.S. Joe said to tell you "Hello"...

Figure 8.2

which is time sensitive. Furthermore, I am also being proactive by following up on the voice-mail I left late last week, and I am specifically asking for a response to see if it makes sense to briefly update her on the details—"Please advise."

There's no magic here. If the recipient of my email wonders, "What two issues?", or, "How will that affect my business?", I will surely get a prompt response.

To glean some specific ideas on what types of things might be most relevant to your customers, I must once again refer you to the exercise I introduced in Chapter 5, where I recommended that you build a repository of potential business issues and implications that could be important to customers. If you completed this assignment already, just take any industry issue and sprinkle in a couple "specifics," and you will be well on your way to a significantly improved response rate, whether you are leaving voice-mail messages or sending emails.

Use Curiosity Throughout the Sales Process

Using specific techniques to leverage curiosity is clearly one of the two most important ingredients in the recipe for engaging new prospects—credibility being the other critical ingredient. If customers are not the least bit curious about what you bring to the table, and they don't believe that you are a credible resource, the sales profession can be a tough way to make a living.

These strategies for leveraging curiosity and establishing credibility are not limited to the introductory part of the sale, however. As you will see in Chapters 9 and 10, when we talk about *Positioning Your Solutions* and *Wrapping Up the Sale*, your ability to build upon similar themes throughout the rest of the sales process will enable you to convey significantly more value and facilitate the closing of sales transactions in a very comfortable buying atmosphere.

Chapter 9

Positioning Your Solutions

Whether you are leading a sales call, working the booth at a trade show, or delivering a product presentation, your ability to effectively position solutions is critical to your success.

Positioning an effective value proposition requires more than just rattling off a bunch of features and benefits, however. To register real value with decision makers, they must conclude that your product's capabilities are the best option to address their needs.

What is the objective of a sales presentation? Are you trying to educate buyers on the potential value of your solutions? Are you also trying to differentiate yourself from the competition? What about justifying the decision to prospective customers? Seasoned sales professionals would have all of these goals in mind.

Solid presentation skills have long been touted as the hinge pin for success in sales. Everyone knows that a good presentation can win you the business, and a sub-par presentation can just as easily set back your efforts to close a sale. If you've ever attended a presentation skills course, however, then you know that most of the instruction tends to focus on style, and the manner in which the material is being presented. While I agree that having a comfortable and effective presentation style is undoubtedly a valuable asset, sellers also need to think about how to position themselves in a way that maximizes the perceived value of their solutions in an increasingly competitive marketplace.

It's difficult to alter someone's personal style, so I am happy to leave your style alone. Instead, let's presume that one of the reasons customers like to deal with you is because of *you*. But, that doesn't mean we should turn a blind eye to positioning logic or what it takes to have a winning presentation strategy.

Once more, we've come to philosophical crossroads in your professional development as a salesperson. For years, sellers have been taught to position themselves and their solutions using an SPA approach, which doesn't necessarily coincide with how buyers process information (PAS). Sorry to rock the boat yet again, but the traditional mindset of conveying value by focusing on the features and benefits of a proposed solution no longer cuts it in a competitive environment.

I don't have a problem with sellers talking about the capabilities of their products. At the appropriate time in the decision cycle, you're supposed to educate prospective buyers on the value of your proposed solutions and set expectations with regard to the benefits they can expect to receive. My worry is that simply running through a list of features and benefits doesn't necessarily translate into perceived value.

One of the common themes throughout this book is the idea that the *actual value* of your product or service is only as great as how it is being perceived by prospective buyers. Even if you represent the most robust and wonderful solution in the world, customers will only buy your product or service if the value perceived is great enough to justify the cost. In addition to being cost effective, you must also prevail over competitive options in order to be selected as vendor of choice.

If your product or company offers some feature/benefit that gives you a whopping technical or functional advantage, and one that customers absolutely need, then by all means, you should exploit your advantage as long as it can be sustained. It's easy (and fun) to sell if your offering is essentially the only game in town. Enjoy it while you can.

If you sell in a competitive market, however, where providers other than you offer comparable solutions, the true differences between your proposal and a competitor's may be much smaller, if not indiscernible. In those cases, the customer's

> "If the outcome of a sale comes down to whoever has the best positioning skills, that gives you an opportunity to control your own destiny."

perception of your value is going to be largely influenced by *how* your solution is being positioned, which brings your positioning strategy into play. To me, this is terrific news, because if the outcome of a sale comes down to whoever has the best positioning skills, that gives you an opportunity to control your own success.

The question we must address from here is: What can you do to put yourself and your products in the strongest possible position to win business? Rather than trying to come up with a magic bullet, however, the rest of this chapter focuses on a number of strategies and presentation nuances that can give you a significant and sustainable positioning advantage.

Battling for Conversational Control

The first topic we must talk about with regard to positioning your products and services is conversational control. If it was totally up to you, who would you rather be in control of your sales conversations, you or the customer? Given the choice, most sellers would absolutely want to be in control, in order to maximize the value of time spent with potential buyers. However, if you asked the typical customer who they would want to control the conversation when dealing with a vendor, you would quickly discover that decision makers aren't always eager to yield the floor to a salesperson.

Suddenly, a battle for control is brewing. Salespeople want to be in control of their conversations with customers, but so does the customer. Who is going to win this battle for control? That depends on the answer to this question: Why is it in the customer's best interest for you to be in control? I ask because I know that if it doesn't benefit the customer for you to be in control of the sales conversation, you probably won't be.

To me, the most important reason to have at least some control over your dialogue is to make good use of the customer's time by keeping the conversation on track. As a salesperson, you should have a pretty clear idea of how you can provide value. So, it stands to reason that if you are able to focus on those areas that are most beneficial to the customer, you will accomplish more than just letting the conversation randomly wander. Whether you get five minutes or two hours in front of a customer, providing maximum value during that window of time is not only good for customers, it also places you in the strongest competitive position.

So, how exactly is a salesperson supposed to control their sales conversations, especially when decision makers are cautious or standoffish? Strangely, the answer to this question comes down to simple punctuation—using questions, not statements.

With most sales presentations, flow is very important. Presumably, you are going to present a logical sequence of ideas and information to support the assertion that customers will be better off by purchasing your product or service, rather than selecting a competitive proposal, or doing nothing. The operative word here is "logical."

Some of your success when delivering an effective sales presentation is content dependent. For our purposes here, let's assume you represent a viable company that offers a robust product or service, and you have a compelling story to tell. Even so, part of what makes any story compelling is the logical flow of the presentation, in terms of how your proposed solution is being justified to your target audience.

If you took a compelling presentation, for example, and you mixed up the delivery sequence, maybe by putting the slides in random order, the effectiveness of your message would be greatly reduced. The opposite is also true. Enhancing the underlying logical flow of your sales presentation can significantly increase the customer's perception of your value.

For now, let's agree that we want our sales presentations to start on track and we also want them to stay on track—not only to maximize our opportunity to sell, but also to make the best use of the customer's time. In addition to just controlling the flow of the presentation, we also want to establish credibility as a valuable resource, lower the decision maker's natural defenses, and make our target audience more receptive to our suggestions and advice. You do all of this by controlling the flow of the conversation with strategic questions.

Whether you are educating a customer on a first time sales call, or you are closing for a commitment at the end of a more formal presentation, you are not only trying to sell your products and services, you are also selling yourself.

Kicking Off Your Sales Presentations

Unless I am dealing with a very large audience, I generally shy away from using formal agendas to kick off my sales presentations. I know, I know...sellers have been taught for years to kick off sales calls and presentations by reviewing their agenda. In some cases, sellers are even encouraged to secure verbal contracts that supposedly commit the audience to spend a predetermined amount of time in the presentation.

The problem with starting off a meeting or presentation by reviewing the agenda is that it's too easily perceived as *your* agenda. Granted, you should come to meetings fully prepared and you should also have a clear picture of what you hope to accomplish. But, it's important to make sure your opening comments sound mutually beneficial as opposed to sounding one-sided or self-serving.

My rule of thumb on sales calls and during product presentations is to save the chit-chat and small talk for the end of the meeting. It's perfectly okay to be professional and courteous. But, especially early in your interactions, customers are sizing you up and forming their initial impressions. First and foremost, they understand that some vendors are more valuable than others. Hence, they will be quietly assessing you to figure out whether you are smart, knowledgeable, capable, competent, trustworthy, and if you are planning to make valuable use of their time. Therefore, I would much rather err on the side of being purposeful and relevant as a means of gaining some early traction with the customer. Just being chatty and convivial doesn't do a lot to prove you're competent or capable.

At the beginning of a sales call, for example, it would be easy for me to say, *"Mr. Customer, I know that you are a busy person, so I'll get to the part that might impact you the most. We have announced two programs in the last five weeks, one of which enables customers to significantly reduce their overhead costs for production and the other we believe can boost your revenue by as much as twenty percent. Would it make sense for me to take a few minutes and bring you up to speed on these?"* Being purposeful upfront makes the customer's decision on whether or not to spend time with me relatively simple. I've figured out if you say something that piques their curiosity, they will absolutely invite you to educate them. Instantly, you have created a more receptive audience. By being forthright and relevant, you have also boosted your credibility. Of course, once the customer grants you permission to fill them in on the details, you are in a good position to say, *"I'd be happy to give you all the details. Can I ask a couple specifics about your...?"* Bingo! You're off and running.

This is the same technique we talked about earlier called *manufacturing a mini-invitation*. Once you are invited to proceed, the customer subtly transfers control of the conversation, either by giving you permission to ask questions, or, in this case, their invitation provides a smooth and seamless transition into your sales presentation. If you had started off with a statement like, "I'm now going to tell you about our products and services," you may still get into your presentation, but you do so at the risk of customers reacting standoffishly to what sounds like a self-serving agenda.

If you are going to present solutions in a more formal setting, like to a decision committee or board of directors, let me offer a few pointers on how best to kick off that type of presentation.

First, I always ask my champion in the account, or whoever scheduled the presentation, to kick off the meeting and introduce the participants. This is especially important when multiple people are involved, because being introduced to the group as an invited guest takes away much of the awkwardness that would otherwise ensue if you just dove into your spiel. I'm not looking for some fabulous introduction, just someone to welcome everyone, communicate the objectives of the meeting, and then turn it over to me.

Once the floor of the meeting is turned over, I usually start by thanking people for their time—not profusely—just enough to signal that I'm aware their time is valuable and to let them know I plan to make a good use of it.

The next thing I do is state the purpose of the meeting. In doing so, my strategy (and my style) is to pull back the proverbial curtain and verbally point at the decision issues the customer currently faces. It's the quickest way to get the group's attention. There's no point in beating around the bush. If a customer wants to know about your solutions, you might as well frame your value proposition by first demonstrating a knowledge of the challenges they face. Let me give you an example of what my introductory comments in a formal presentation might actually sound like.

Seller: *"Thank you everyone for your time. I know we're coming up on your busy season, so I'll jump right in. Over the past several weeks, I have met with a number of people regarding your IT implementation and I think I have a decent understanding of your objectives. Although I don't know everything about your business, I have done some homework in advance of this meeting and I put together several options for your consideration.*

Frankly, there are a couple of ways we can do this. If you like, I would be happy to deliver a standard marketing pitch. We have plenty of slides and glossies and I can ramble on with the best of them. Or, we could put the canned sales pitch aside, roll up our sleeves, and have a more specific conversation about your goals and objectives for this project.

Let me ask the group, which would you rather I do?"

As you can see, my style is straightforward, direct, and hopefully, highly professional. Most importantly, customers are visibly relieved when they realize that you actually have something valuable to say.

The next thing that happens is critical—I pause and wait for someone to answer my question. What I'm really looking for is a mini-invitation from the audience. Invariably, someone in the meeting will say, *"Great, let's get specific and talk about the project."* Others in the room will nod and think to themselves, *"I'm glad this isn't just another vendor pitch."* You can literally see people lean forward in their chairs with a sense of anticipation, once you have clearly signaled you are headed down a different path than most.

Notice that I didn't just open it up to the audience by asking what they'd like me to cover, or how they wanted the presentation to go. I simply offered them a choice, either for me to deliver a standard marketing pitch or facilitate a more productive working session. Of course, I already knew which option they would choose, mostly because of the way my question was phrased. I subtly poisoned one of the options knowing that nobody wants a 'standard pitch.'

Once you get invited by the customer to get specific, it's very natural then to say, *"Well, can I ask the group a couple specifics about your _____?"* Invariably, they'll say, "Yes." Notice how this formal presentation has suddenly has turned conversational.

The same technique that we used to kick off the needs development conversation (*Diagnostic Questions*) provides a perfect jumping off point in your sales presentations as well. But, since you've already done your homework and prepared for the presentation in advance, you can now do more than just gather information. You can leverage this same strategy of narrowing the *Scope* of your questions to demonstrate competence, earn credibility, and verify that the information you have based your recommendations on is indeed correct.

Here's how that might sound.

Seller: *"My understanding from talking with Dave and Terry is that you currently support approximately 125 employees across four locations. Correct?" (they nod yes) "And, while most of these people have similar desktop computers, their application mix differs from user to user...right?" (more nodding) "And, the short term*

*objective is to implement a consistent technology plat-
form across the organization within the next sixty
days, yes?"*

In Question Based Selling, we say, "He who asks the questions controls the conversation." It's one of those immutable
laws of nature. By first securing the customer's permission to
proceed, it's easy to earn the right to ask a series of diagnostic
questions. This enables you to initiate an interactive dialogue
with the audience. From there, it's a simple transition into needs
development, where you can either explore or confirm a
customer's issues and the implications of those issues.

Think about it this way. The only reason a customer would
want to sit through a vendor's presentation is to understand how
the vendor's solutions match up to their needs. That said, the
best way to facilitate this matching exercise is to roll up your
sleeves, and facilitate a more in-depth conversation that begins
with some confirmation of what you understand to be the
customer's needs.

Confirming a Mutual Agenda

Kicking your sales presentations off in a productive direction is good, but you must continue to escalate the dialogue to
reach the intended level of depth and mutual value. Ultimately,
sellers want to talk with customers about their problems, goals,
issues, concerns, needs, wants, and desires. The challenge is,
getting those problems and issues on the table for discussion
sometimes requires a little finesse. Just telling people what their
problems are at the beginning of your presentations could

sound presumptuous. You risk putting people off. Doing the opposite, and thinking that you will engage in a nice long needs development conversation, eats into your time to educate the customer, particularly if you are there to "present" solutions.

Most corporate presentations have a preferred, logical flow. Through trial and error and real-life experiences, presentations have been meticulously crafted to follow an agenda that should maximize the seller's probability of success. The trick is getting people to buy into your agenda, early in the delivery, so you can then present your product in its best light. To secure the necessary buy in from your presentation audiences, try making your agenda their agenda.

First you secure permission to have a "roll up your sleeves" discussion about details, versus a generic overview. Then you kick off the interaction by asking a series of diagnostic questions to verify the status of the account, and also to establish your own credibility. Next, like we talked about in needs development, you want to get the customer's issues on the table for discussion. This becomes an exercise in facilitation. You bring up topics that you know are important to the customer (having done your homework in advance), in order to articulate and frame the customer's problem.

Seller: *"Richard, several issues came up during our last conversation, including: Growth, Security, Uptime, Training, Cost Effectiveness, Support, Upgrades, and Performance. The options I put together for you would provide benefits in each of these areas. Is there anything else that we need to include on the list of business issues?*

As the facilitator of the meeting, be sure to write each of the issues you bring up on a flipchart or whiteboard, or even on a piece of paper. This gives the customer a chance to see where you are headed and it also gives them an opportunity to elaborate on any specific concerns they might like you to address in your presentation.

*Growth
*Security
*Uptime
*Training
*Support
*Upgrades
*Performance

As a way to uncover any hidden concerns customers may have, I always ask, *"Is there anything else you would like me to cover?"* If so, simply add it onto the bottom of your list. If not, the customer will say, "No, that's pretty much it for now."

Suddenly, you have created a perfect agenda for your presentation. Whose agenda is it? By leading the audience down a question-based path from the onset, and involving them in the development or verification of issues that are important to them, you will have created a *mutual agenda*. But, since you were the one who facilitated the discussion, you get to control the sequence of your presentation by raising issues in the order that best suits your message.

This notion of proactively raising a customer's issues should look familiar. Do you remember back in Chapter 2 when we talked about differentiating yourself in a job interview? Again, an employment interview is the ultimate product presentation, where you are totally responsible for selling yourself. That being the case, if you are able to facilitate a more in-depth conversation about the customer's goals and your solutions, you are in a stronger position to make valid recommendations.

Here's what the product presentation on your next job interview might sound like. "*In addition to being a good person and having a track record of success, my guess (Mr./Ms Hiring Manager) is that you might be looking for more than that—some of the intangibles that don't necessarily show up as line items on a resume. For example, you might want someone who can ramp up quickly, blend in with the existing culture but also bring some fresh ideas to the team, diffuse tough account situations, and perpetuate solid relationships, etc...*"

This is classic PAS positioning, and it's just as appropriate in a presentation as it is in a sales call or job interview. After all, you are attempting to do the same thing in all three scenarios—match your solutions up to the customer's needs. In order for someone to be ready and willing to make a purchase decision, they must conclude the following. They must say to themselves, "*Because I have certain problems, issues, goals, needs, and requirements, that other alternatives don't address as effectively, that's why I choose to purchase your solution (PAS).*" When you establish a mutual agenda that accurately reflects the customer's goals, you put yourself in a strong position to effectively facilitate a discussion about how your offerings compare favorably to other alternatives the customer might also be considering.

Let me alert you to one common mistake that can easily be made. It's generally not a good idea to kick off your sales presentations by asking, "What do you want me to cover today?" This is a strategic miss because it does not communicate that you have a reasonable understanding of the customer's goals and objectives or that you are prepared. Inviting your presentation audience to take you off on any random tangent is a sure way to end up with mayhem in the conference room.

The Feature/Benefit Presentation is Dead

If the feature/benefit presentation isn't already dead, it is definitely on life support. Your next prospect might even say it this way, "If I have to sit through another boring, generic sales presentation, I will probably hang myself."

For as long as I have been in sales, the feature/benefit presentation has been largely regarded as the recommended way to sell. I suppose it's natural for sellers to want to describe all the wonderful features of their products, and then explain how those features will benefit customers. As with many long-standing practices, people sometimes argue that positioning features and benefits is the way to go because that's how everyone else does it. I say, sounding like everyone else doesn't give you a viable differentiation strategy. In fact, how you choose to position yourself in future opportunities might depend on the answer to one simple question: Would you rather be perceived by potential buyers as more of a 'solutions provider' or a 'problem solver?'

> "For some reason, "We provide solutions," has become the standard battle cry of the insanely average businessperson."

For the last fifteen years or so, the idea of 'providing solutions' has been bantered back and forth between professional marketing departments like a corporate shuttlecock. For some reason, "We provide solutions," has become the standard battle cry of the insanely average businessperson.

Is that what customers really want—your solutions? Earlier, I asked: what is more important to the typical customer, their problems or your solutions? If you agree that customers are much more interested in their own problems, issues, and concerns, than they are in the salesperson's agenda, then it seems to me we should align our value proposition with the customer's primary focus (solving problems) and not the vendor's primary focus (selling solutions.)

Customers in all industries are much more worried about achieving their own goals than trying to help a corporate sales organization achieve their sales quota. Consequently, I would much rather be seen as a *problem solver*, rather than jumping on the same bandwagon as every other seller over the last twenty years who thinks they are differentiating themselves by running around selling "solutions."

If it's true that becoming a trusted advisor is the ideal position for a salesperson to be in, then we might want to pause long enough to realize that customers who want advice are dealing with actual problems, not just solutions.

Are we just splitting hairs with semantics? Isn't the act of solving a problem and the act of providing a solution one in the same? Yes, that's true. A salesperson can't solve a problem without providing a solution. Likewise, providing a solution is only beneficial if it actually solves a problem.

But, if you think about it, the only real reason for a salesperson to call on customers is to help them solve a problem of some kind. Surprisingly, most vendors position themselves in a way that is essentially opposite from this. In the feature/benefit model, you basically tell customers about some cool feature of *your* product, and then relate it to how it might benefit *them*. Thus, an SPA approach creates a logic problem for sellers because it's backwards from how most customers make decisions.

PAS is much more effective as a positioning strategy not only because it aligns with the decision process, it's also the most effective way to educate customers on the value of intangible benefits. Remember, in order for someone to purchase your product or service, they must conclude the following: Because we have a problem (P), that the alternatives (A) don't address as effectively, that's why we choose to purchase your solution (S). So, rather than pointing out features of your product and explaining why they're good for customers, it's more effective to use the opposite approach. Because customers face certain problems that competing alternatives do not address as effectively, that's essentially what we solve (PAS).

Most Buyers are Comparative Thinkers

When we talk about PAS positioning, it's easy to focus much of your energy on understanding the customer's problem (P), and positioning the corresponding value of your solutions (S). But, don't forget to spend time with potential customers about (A)— the alternatives to purchasing your product or service.

I assume most of the people who are reading this book sell in a competitive environment. If that's true, then it's also safe to assume that your prospects and customers are going to look at or consider other options besides your own.

Most decision makers are comparative shoppers. I am, and you probably are as well. Granted, I won't visit every store in the area to compare prices or products, but I usually explore my options before pulling the trigger on an important purchase. This includes exploring the option to do nothing or maintain the status quo.

If you are the only vendor that can offer solutions and your customer has to make an immediate decision, then you may not even need a sales strategy. However, this level of exclusivity is rarely the case. Most buyers will consider options other than yours in an effort to make the best decision. That's where your role as a salesperson comes into play. If you aren't proactive in helping customers compare and contrast the different alternatives being considered, then your competitors probably will be. You have to figure that decision makers are going to turn to someone for advice. And, since you are the most equipped to position your products against competitive offerings, then it's in your best interest (and the customer's) for you to lead that conversation. Don't leave it to a competitor or hope it doesn't come up. Put it this way. If I was competing against you and you left the comparison of our products to me, I would gladly eat your lunch.

I actually look for opportunities to bring up alternatives (A) when talking with potential buyers. The logic is simple. Given that most customers will consider options other than mine anyway, I want to at least be involved in the discussion. Moreover, I'm always looking for opportunities to speed up the sales process. If we can compare and contrast the various options upfront, that could even knock some vendors out of contention before the actual decision process begins.

I never bring up or bad mouth a competitive vendor by name. I figure my competition has their own marketing departments and it's not my job to introduce them into prospect accounts. Let them find their own leads. However, if a customer asks me to compare and contrast my offering to a competitors', then it's 'game on' and I'm definitely ready to position my strengths against their weaknesses. Still, I don't talk badly about them. Mud-slinging usually backfires anyway, because it makes the person who's doing the bad-mouthing sound defensive.

Ultimately, you want to facilitate a comparative thought process that differentiates you from the competition in the customer's mind. You do this in part by demonstrating your knowledge of the customer's problem (P). You also want to increase the customer's comfort level that they are indeed making the right choice, thus widening the separation that exists between your offering and other alternatives (A). I like to call it *subtly poisoning*. Let me show you what this sounds like in the context of what I sell—strategic sales training. Listen for the (P) as I characterize the problem, and then the alternatives (A):

Freese: *"Mr. Sales Executive, if you want to increase revenue, shorten the sales process, and strengthen your position in the marketplace, you basically have a couple of options. One alternative would be to simply continue with your current approach, although that would likely produce the same results.*

A second alternative would be to hire one of the name brand training companies to come in and redefine your sales process. The challenge is, just "defining" the sales process doesn't address the real problem. I bet your people don't need a refresher course explaining that Step 1 in the sales process is 'Identify New Opportunities,' Step 2 is to 'Qualify,' Step 3 is to 'Uncover Needs, and so on. They've already been schooled on "what" to do. So have your competitors.

Rather than just redefining the process, QBS actually solves a different problem. Because most sellers already know what the steps in the process are, Question Based Selling is a methodology for teaching salespeople "how" to execute more effectively. If you look around any sales organization, you will see that some salespeople are more effective than others, selling the same products to the same types of customers. But, instead of making each person figure out how to boost their own results, we essentially shorten the development cycle by showing sellers how to realign their strategy in ways that will greatly improve sales results.

Did you hear me bad mouth anyone else's training program? No. In fact, I didn't mention any other program by name. I did, however, plant a few seeds of doubt that might dampen the customer's enthusiasm for pursuing a "refresher course." In essence, I made the point that continuing with the current approach probably wouldn't accomplish the client's goals of improving revenue or gaining marketshare. And I pointed out that redefining the sales process won't make your salespeople more effective than your competitors. Both things are true, which is what makes QBS so different. It's also why we spend a fair amount of time 'undoing' what sellers have been taught over the last twenty-five years.

Tell a Story in Your Sales Presentations

The best piece of sales advice I ever received was from my sales manager and mentor, Barry Gillman, back in 1992. I had just accepted a position selling NetFrame Superservers into an emerging market and very few people had even heard about our technology. Barry, my boss and a seasoned technology guy told me, *"Tom, when you present solutions to a customer, if you take the time to say it, be sure and also take the time to explain it."*

In sales, you need to have a good story to tell. Presumably, you represent a viable company that offers valuable solutions, so the easiest part of telling your product's story is rattling off the various bullet points that comprise your value proposition. I'm sure you have access to brochures, handouts, PowerPoint slides, or other marketing aids that enhance your presentation. But, it's not enough just to "have" a good story; you also have to tell it in a way that conveys the full extent of your value.

The key to explaining your value proposition in its most valuable terms is *translation*. In addition to mentioning key points in your presentation, you also have to explain how your product or service will impact the customer, and translate that into real value for them. This can happen in two ways. Customers must either figure out for themselves how you provide value, or you (as the advice giver) must be proactive enough to help them recognize the value of your offering—essentially, by connecting the dots. My preference is to be a 'dot connector,' mostly because I want to make sure key points that get made during my presentation will positively impact the customer's perception of my value.

If you built a repository of business issues and implications to facilitate your needs development conversations, it can also serve as a comprehensive guide for translating value during your sales presentations. The repository itself is basically a physical list of "what" issues are important to potential buyers, and "why" those issues might be important. The salesperson's job (as translator) is to map the capabilities of your solution back to how it actually impacts the customer—implications. Just like we decided that depth of conversation was your friend during needs development, depth of conversation is equally valuable when it comes to positioning your solutions.

To illustrate, suppose you took your newfound insight from this book and embarked on a new career selling umbrellas. We talked about the real value of owning an umbrella earlier. I'm sure your umbrellas would protect people form the rain. The brochure that comes with the umbrella might even point out that it helps the person standing underneath to avoid getting wet. But, I would want to take the opportunity to educate potential customers, by pointing out that our umbrellas would protect their clothes (a silk tie or leather jacket), and it also would help protect them from catching a cold, possibly getting sick, and unnecessarily having to miss work. I might also make the point that it's important for people look their best if they are meeting a client or someone special after work.

Students in our live training courses sometimes ask, "Tom, couldn't the umbrella salesperson in the next kiosk say the same things about their products?" The answer is, sure they could, but only if they are as strategic as you. My strategy is simple and repeatable. Just ask yourself, how many reasons do you want customers to have to buy from you? More implications translates into more reasons to buy from *you*, and giving customers more reasons to buy (from me) is clearly my strategy to win more sales in an otherwise highly competitive environment.

Note that the goal when delivering a value proposition isn't necessarily to make the prospect an expert on every facet of your product or service. You don't have to teach customers how to be attorneys to sell legal services. Similarly, the fact that I don't understand all the engineering behind how an automobile engine actually works does not negate my desire or ability to purchase a well built automobile. My goal during a sales presentation is simply to convey enough value for customers to make a sound business decision, and to build enough credibility for decision makers to feel confident they are dealing with someone who understands their needs and will support them after the sale.

Positioning Yourself During a Job Interview

We already know the first question during a job interview. At the appropriate time, the hiring manager will say, "Tell me about yourself." A similar thing happens during sales calls, when a customer asks, "What are you selling?"

As we saw in the interview scenario from Chapter 2, most candidates simply answer the question. They think, "This person wants to know more about me, so by golly, I'm going to tell him." Honestly, my first instinct now is to do the exact opposite. Rather than rattle off a bunch of selling points about myself, maybe what the hiring manager really wants to know is, am I customer-focused or self-centered? Or, what if the interviewer is thinking, 'I wonder to what extent this candidate really understands our organization, or my needs'. If the customer (or hiring manager) is truly focused on their own agenda rather than your pitch about yourself, then your best strategy when selling yourself may be to actually focus on them.

Again, I'm not trying to dodge the interviewer's question. I just want to position myself (and my services) in a manner that gives my target audience the clearest picture for how I might be able to provide the most value for them.

Remember the dialogue?

Manager: *"Dale, thanks for meeting with me today. Can you tell me a little about yourself?"*

Candidate: *"Since you already have my work history, I would add that I am a hard working person with a decent track record. But, my guess is you may be looking for more than that to fill this position—perhaps some of the intangibles that don't always show up as specific line items on a resume.*

For example, I'm guessing that in addition to finding someone with knowledge and experience, you would want someone who could ramp up and become productive as quickly as possible. You might also be looking for someone who can blend well with the current culture, but who can also contribute new ideas and possibly a fresh perspective to the team. As long as we're hypothesizing, you may also be looking for someone with a positive attitude, who is self-motivated and extremely customer-focused."

Our hero in this interview scenario raises several issues that are likely to be hot buttons for the hiring manager—including, ramp up time, productivity, cultural blending, fresh ideas, and having the right attitude. At a minimum, this candidate is demonstrating that he is indeed customer-focused and does have some understanding about what might be important to the hiring manager and the host company.

Over the course of a thirty or sixty minute interview, there will be plenty of opportunity to tell about your background, experiences, work history, education, and personal life. Just remember that the points you mention need to be translated into why those things would be valuable for the customer—in this case, the hiring manager.

For example, as you tell about your college years or work experiences, be sure to relate how the lessons you learned will enable you to ramp up more quickly, and bring a new perspective or a fresh set of ideas to the team. If the interviewer asks you to tell about a challenge you've faced and how you overcame it (a popular interviewing question), I would cite an example that seems appropriate, but I would also make the point that dealing with these types of challenges has given me a positive attitude and a better appreciation for dealing with other people.

Always remember that decision makers are not so concerned about your resume during a job interview, just as customers don't really care what's printed on the product brochure during a sales call. What potential buyers are interested in is how those details will affect your performance in the job, and how you will help them accomplish their goals. Recognizing this will make you exponentially more effective when it comes to selling yourself and positioning the value of your solutions.

> "Decision makers are not so concerned about your resume during a job interview, just as customers don't really care what's printed on the product brochure during a sales call."

Chapter 10

Wrapping Up the Sale

Closing a sale is relatively simple once you reach the point where your customer is ready to move forward with a purchase. If a decision maker is not convinced that purchasing your product or service is the right thing, however, then more selling needs to occur.

Since a sales transaction usually represents the culmination of several smaller victories on the way to closing the larger sale, a savvy salesperson can revisit many of the same strategies and techniques used earlier in the sales process to close more deals.

What's the best way to increase the number of transactions you close per month, per quarter, or per year? One way is to treat sales as a numbers game and try to increase the number of opportunities coming into the pipeline. Another way to boost the bottom line is to focus on those things that will secure more mindshare from key decision makers within target accounts. You can also help yourself by expanding your needs development conversations to include a broader range of issues and implications, in order to differentiate yourself from the competition. Of course, you would also want to implement the positioning skills we just talked about in Chapter 9, to maximize the customer's perception of your value. Doing all of these things should put you in good shape to close more deals. So, let's talk more specifically about your role in wrapping up the sale.

Honestly, the act of closing a sale should be an anticlimactic event. If a client clearly sees the value of your product or service and agrees that your solutions will address important needs, wrapping up a sales transaction shouldn't be any more difficult than just saying, "Press hard, five copies." However, if the customer does not recognize the value of your solutions, using manipulative techniques or closing gimmicks is probably not going to help.

As far as I'm concerned, you can take all the books, tapes, and training videos that claim to offer "sure-fire" closing tricks and throw them in the trash—every last one of them. If your customer truly *wants* to move forward with a purchase, then you don't need tricks to wrap up a transaction. And, in those cases where a customer (for whatever reason) is not yet comfortable enough to move forward, I would argue that the sale is not ready to be closed. Ask yourself, what trick can a salesperson use in today's business climate to make you buy something you don't really want?

The real "trick" to being successful in sales is causing customers to visualize how your solutions will address their needs, and thus make them comfortable enough to justify a decision to purchase. So far, much of our focus has been on filling the pipeline, securing mindshare, conveying value, and differentiating yourself from the competition. Now, it is time to *pull back the curtains* on the end of the sales process and focus on what you can do to expedite customer decisions and wrap up more sales.

Find Out Where You Stand

I have never considered myself to be a pushy salesperson. I am forthright and direct with people, but not pushy. Maybe it's because I don't appreciate being pushed when I'm the customer, especially not by some salesperson who seems more intent on achieving their own goals than helping me achieve mine.

A point will come in every sale, however, where the buyer must choose whether or not to move forward with a purchase. At the same time, sellers must decide whether or not to continue pursuing the opportunity, and if so, how best to proceed in a way that's not pushy, but still mutually beneficial.

Still, the end of the sales process is notorious for creating awkward moments between salespeople and their customers. Potential buyers are well aware that you want to close the deal, so there's no point in being timid. It's perfectly acceptable for a salesperson to have goals. But, invariably the moment of truth will arrive, where you are either going to find out that your efforts will be rewarded with the completion of a sale, or you will learn that the customer has decided to go in some other direction. Essentially, that's the point where a salesperson feels like they are putting their neck on the block and hoping that it doesn't get chopped off.

Recently I heard a sales executive quote a statistic saying that seventy-eight percent of all salespeople hesitate when it comes to asking for the order. I believe it, knowing that the risk of rejection is the single largest demotivator in the entire sales profession. Even so, sellers must find a way ask for the order, because it's the only way to know where your customer actually stands relative to making a purchase. It's also the only way to know how best to pursue the opportunity from there.

Putting the awkwardness of the situation aside, closing is really about getting an accurate status on where you stand in the sales process. Is the customer ready to move forward with a purchase? If not, what is holding them back? Are there sticking points or outstanding issues that still need to be addressed? Does anyone else need to be involved in the decision?

Knowing the true status of the sale is the only way a salesperson can know how best to proceed. Ever had an objection come up in the eleventh hour of a deal, that you were able to successfully address and still complete the transaction? I have experienced this many times. No one wants customers to raise objections, but it's definitely true that you can't address obstacles you don't know about. Sound logic and good closing techniques, therefore, become valuable tools for the proactive salesperson who strives to manage their sales opportunities all the way through closure, as opposed to just letting sales situations play out on their own.

If you discover that one or more of the opportunities you have in the pipeline is not going to happen, my philosophy is that it's better to find out sooner rather than later to avoid chasing phantom deals on your sales forecast. Frankly, this level of insight enables a realistic salesperson to redeploy their time, effort, and resources to focus on other more legitimate opportunities. Finding out that the customer *is* ready to move forward with a purchase is equally important, so you can get on with the details of wrapping up the transaction.

There are several schools of thought on the best way to actually pop the closing question. Much of it is situational and will depend of the context of your conversation, the mix of personalities involved, and your relationship with the customer. I purposely use the phrase, "closing question," because as you've probably noticed, I'm not very good at pussy-footing around. I would rather be direct and to the point, knowing that an effective question-based approach gives me the best chance to achieve the desired result, with the least amount of risk.

When you aren't sure exactly where you stand at the end of the sales process, trying to somehow guess what to do next is a high-risk sales strategy. Should you give the client some more time to make a decision, or allow them enough distance to get comfortable with your proposal? Or, would it be better to show some initiative and recommend more strongly that they should move forward now? Would a price discount provide enough incentive to act, or would that just end up eroding your profit margin? When is it appropriate to take a customer to lunch or dinner, and do those events obligate decision makers in key accounts to buy in anyway? Because it's so easy to guess wrong, sellers who just take shots in the dark end up making preventable mistakes, like unnecessarily discounting their price or wasting valuable sales resources.

To me, the best way to find out where you stand in the sale is to put your closing question in hypothetical terms. After you have identified the customer's needs and have educated them on your value proposition, you simply summarize the progression of events that brought the decision process to this point. Then you simply ask them if it "makes sense" to take the appropriate next step. Here's how that sounds in an actual dialogue.

Seller: *"Mr. Customer, given that you are looking to improve manufacturing efficiency, cut costs, and preserve quality,* *which is exactly what this product provides, would it make sense to move forward with the contract in order for you to begin realizing the benefits of our solutions?"*

The phrase, "Would it make sense to...," is particularly effective when suggesting possible next steps in the decision process. We talked about this briefly in Chapter 4, in the context of *Managing Conversational Dynamics* and securing mini-invitations. The phrase, *"Would it make sense...,"* essentially brings logic into play, suggesting that the reason to move forward is to benefit the customer. That takes away any sense that you're focused on raking in a commission. Whether it does or does not "make sense" for the customer to take your suggested next step, asking in a way that's forthright and direct gives you the opportunity to find out where you stand, so you can either wrap up the terms of the sale or work with customers to resolve any outstanding issues.

> "The only legitimate reason to move forward with a transaction is because your product or service most effectively addresses the customer's need."

I usually recommend that sellers avoid older school closing euphemisms like, "Can we shake on it?", or, "Do we have a deal?", because they tend to sound sales-y and self-serving. Customers know you probably stand to earn some sort of bonus or commission from the transaction, but a salesperson's income doesn't ever justify a purchase. In fact, the only legitimate reason to consummate a transaction is because yours is the product or service that most effectively addresses the customer's need.

Trial Close for a Softer Touch

I personally don't like the idea of twisting a customer's arm to try and close a sale. The last thing I want to do is forge a strong relationship with prospective clients and then create an awkward situation at the end of the sale by closing too aggressively.

It's a balancing act—sellers must be forthright enough to find out where they stand in the sale and know how best to proceed, but there isn't any upside to being harsh, pushy, or manipulative at the end of the decision cycle.

One way to minimize your risk of sounding aggressive is to use trial closes. A *trial close* is a question that gives you a gentler way to be direct, sensitive, and respectful during that part of the decision where customers often don't want to be pressured. Trial closing is essentially a risk reduction strategy. Rather than putting your neck on the block and hoping it doesn't get chopped off, you simply ask something like:

Seller: *"Ms. Prospect, now that you have a pretty complete perspective regarding our products, would it make sense for us to think about sitting down and wrapping up the details?"*

If you notice in the dialogue, the salesperson's trial closing question isn't actually asking the customer to commit to moving forward with a purchase. He is simply asking if it "makes sense" to "think about" sitting down. The prospect's response will generally tell you where they stand. If they agree that, "Yes, it does make sense for us to sit down and wrap up the details," then moving forward with a transaction is relatively easy. On the other hand, if the customer responds cautiously, or for whatever reason, suggests that it doesn't even make sense for them to "think about" sitting down, then you probably aren't close to making a sale. At that point, I would be inclined to say to the customer, "Something's not right, is it?" If something is indeed holding them back, getting the obstacle out in the open can be a relief to the customer, and it accomplishes your objective of knowing where you stand in the sale.

The advantage of a trial close versus going for the jugular is that customers tend to respond more openly when you take a softer approach. More information is always better with regard to closing sales transactions. And, it's always easier to navigate this otherwise sensitive area of asking for a commitment when the customer "wants to" share information with you. With most customers, if they even get so much as a whiff of aggression from an eager salesperson, their defenses will quickly go up and you're back to guessing how best to proceed.

Trial closes are also valuable tools for assessing the validity of potential deals on your sales forecast. Managing the pipeline is important to salespeople and managers, both. And, depending on your industry and the type of products you sell, sales cycles can range from a simple one-call close to a much more complex, multi-faceted decision process that can span several weeks or months. Does your deal have a thirty percent chance of closing, or an eighty percent? What is the likelihood of closing a transaction this month, or within the current quarter? What is the customer's approval process? Who else in the account needs to sign off on the PO? Are there any next steps? Is there anything that can be done to accelerate the purchase?

One of the ways to avoid sounding like a money-grubber is by focusing on the broader decision, and not just the impending purchase. For example, I might ask, "What is the administrative process for this type of decision?" Asking about the "typical" decision process tends to lighten the conversation and minimize any pressure that the customer might be feeling about an impending transaction. Even if a specific deal is up in the air, customers can still talk abstractly about the *typical* administrative process for this *type* of decision.

Sellers must also be sensitive to the fact that large decisions can overwhelm people, thus creating emotional hurdles that can stymie a decision process. Asking trial closing questions is a good way to help customers not feel so overwhelmed. Essentially, it's a divide and conquer strategy, where sellers test a customer's 'readiness' by focusing on smaller aspects of the larger sale. For example, you might ask, *"Mr. Customer, have you talked to your bank about financing?"* Or, *"Where are you planning to warehouse the equipment once it arrives?"* You could ask, *"Have you thought about when you would like to take delivery?"* If the buyer has already talked to the bank, and they already have a plan for where to warehouse the equipment when it arrives, then you are probably in very good shape to move forward.

A medical equipment salesperson, for example, could ask a doctor, *"Do you have any surgery cases scheduled in the next week to ten days?"* An advertising salesperson could ask, *"How far along is the art design for your upcoming advertising campaign?"* A real estate agent might ask a prospective homeowner, *"Have you thought about how you might furnish the kitchen in this particular house?"* Put it this way. If the potential buyer of a house hasn't even "thought about" how it would be furnished, then you probably aren't close to making a sale. On the other hand, if they've already measured for a new dining room suite, that's a good indication that they are close to moving forward with a purchase.

Humbling Disclaimers

Sellers are always encouraged to ask some very specific qualifying questions—to identify key players, understand their timeframe for decision, and to find out if the customer has budget money to spend. Most salespeople understand, however, that a fine line exists between being appropriate in your efforts to qualify an opportunity and sounding invasive by probing for too much information. Moreover, if a customer chooses not to share specific information with you about the opportunity, this puts you at a competitive disadvantage, because you have to assume they must be sharing those details with someone else.

To minimize the risk of being shut down by potential buyers and maximize the amount and quality of information you receive, you can add a precursor of sorts to desensitize your more delicate questions using *humbling disclaimers*. A *humbling disclaimer* is a question-based technique whereby the asker verbally acknowledges the sensitivity of their question in order to proactively diffuse any invasive feelings that could otherwise come from asking probative questions. That's a lot of words, I know, so let me give you an example.

Inquiring about the budget is a good example. Sellers always want to know about the customer's budget. Does the customer have money to spend? Is this deal even worth pursuing? Is there a certain timeframe in which they can spend the money? Understanding the customer's budget requirements is one of the most important qualifying criteria in any pending sales transaction. But just because a salesperson wants to ask about the budget, doesn't necessarily mean customers will openly share this type of information. Consequently, salespeople often end up going back to their managers saying, "I asked about the budget, but the customer is playing it close to the vest."

Should we be surprised that customers are reluctant to share budget information with a salesperson? Picture yourself standing in a car dealership admiring a shiny new sports car on the showroom floor, when an eager salesperson scurries over and asks, "How much money have you got?" I bet you aren't eager to share your W2 or credit score with someone you don't know or trust. Still, sellers are expected to find out about the budget, but when customers don't always share, everyone gets frustrated.

The customer's natural reluctance to share budget details tees up a perfect example of how to use a *humbling disclaimer.* Note that budget usually isn't the first question I'd ask in a sales call, but the time will come when it's appropriate to bring it up in the conversation. When you reach that point in the dialogue, you simply say: "Mr. Customer, I don't want to step out-of-bounds and bring up something I'm not supposed to ask about, but do you mind if I ask the budget question?"

Technically, the answer to my question is either, "Yes," you can ask about the budget, or, "No," you may not. However, when you precede your question with a humbling disclaimer, it's uncanny how often people will open right up and start sharing their financial landscape relative to the purchase. In essence, the humility that's built into your disclaimer disarms the customer even before you deliver your question. Can you see why we call this technique a *humbling disclaimer?*

Of course, your customer could respond to this question by saying, "Yes, you can ask me about the budget, but I'm not going to share details with you." At that point, you weren't going to get specific information about their budget no matter what you had asked. But, don't give up. It's better to get some information rather than no information. I would probably follow up my original question by saying, *"That's fine, Mr. Customer. I understand that budget information is often confidential. But, could I ask you this? If we put together a proposal that ended up being in the forty to fifty-thousand dollar range, do you have the ability to pull the trigger on that type of purchase, or do we need to be thinking about some other approval process?"* Even if a customer doesn't share specific budget data with you, they'll generally give you some indication of whether or not they are able to approve an expenditure, and where you stand relative to that approval process.

Humbling disclaimers are similarly effective when it comes to expanding your needs development conversations. Have you ever asked so many questions that you started to feel yourself running out of runway? The customer's responses get progressively shorter as their indulgence wanes and a sense of impatience creeps into the conversation. When a customer starts to feel they are being "probed" for information, you basically have two options. One is to cut off the needs development discussion and jump immediately into your value proposition. The other option is to say something that creates a longer runway in the conversation. You can easily do this using a *humbling disclaimer.*

Here's an example.

You say, "Mr. Customer, I appreciate you explaining the current manufacturing process and your upcoming re-engineering initiative. And, while I don't want to seem presumptuous by asking too many questions, I would like to understand how these projects could impact your longer-term growth plans. Do you mind if I ask a couple of specifics about your long-range strategy?"

Here are some other examples of humbling disclaimers:

Seller: *"I'm not sure the best way to ask, but would you mind if..."*
"Without stepping on anyone's toes, could I ask about..."
"I don't want to say the wrong thing, but would it be okay..."

To fully appreciate the strategy of using *humbling disclaimers,* I'll let you in on a little secret about human nature. If you are verbally respectful of someone else's right to *not* share information with you, it's amazing how much information you can get. Humility is a very attractive human quality, and one that people are naturally drawn toward. Thus, you can significantly enhance the value of the responses from the questions you ask by strategically preceding your most sensitive questions with a humbling disclaimer. Simply put, causing people to "want to" share more information with

> "If you are respectful of someone else's right to *not* share information with you, it's amazing how much information you can get."

you gives you a strategic advantage over other sellers who are just out there probing for needs.

Neutralize the Disposition of Your Questions

When the time comes to wrap up the details of a sale, the salesperson naturally hopes everything will go well. Perhaps that's why sellers have a tendency to ask hopeful questions, with a certain positive disposition. I introduced this phenomenon in my first book, *Secrets of Question Based Selling*. Sellers tend to ask positive questions in the hopes of receiving a more positive response. It's subconscious, but especially easy to do if your livelihood is contingent on receiving good news from potential buyers.

What do I mean by hopeful questions? And, what exactly does a positively dispositioned sales question sound like? Let me show you a few examples:

Seller: *"Would next Tuesday work for a conference call?"*
"Does your boss like our proposal?"
"Do you think we're still in good shape to wrap this deal up by the end of the month?"

If you try saying any of these questions aloud, you can literally feel your head bobbing up and down as you speak. That positive undertone usually happens as the result of the fact that the deliverer of the question is hoping to receive a positive response.

It turns out that asking hopeful sales questions is a bad strategy. Soliciting only good news tends to reduce the amount of information people share, and it also degrades the accuracy of that information. Let me ask: if a problem is brewing somewhere within one of your accounts, would you want to know about it? Granted, no one wants problems to arise in their sales opportunities, but if something is indeed happening in one of my accounts, I absolutely want to know. An issue can only be successfully addressed if you realize it's happening. That's why I don't ask "hopeful" questions.

Delivering bad news is understandably difficult, particularly when the message being conveyed is not something the other person would necessarily want to hear. Buyers are often put in this situation, especially when they are dealing with an enthusiastic salesperson whose livelihood depends on making sales. In the real world, it's quite possible that a decision maker is not "ready to move forward by the end of the month." Perhaps their budget has been slashed, or the decision committee is leaning toward a competitor's product. Whatever the reason, if bad news is brewing, prospects are often reluctant to share information when they know it's obviously something the salesperson would not want to hear.

> If you want to know where you stand in your accounts, then you must be open to hearing good news and bad news.

If you are in sales and you do want to know where you stand in your accounts, then you must be open to hearing good news and bad news. That's why in Question Based Selling, we teach sellers to *neutralize the disposition* of their sales questions.

Every question that gets asked has a certain "personality" or disposition that can be characterized as being either positive, negative, or neutral. The purpose of neutralizing your questions is to solicit more accurate information about the status of your opportunities, which requires a proactive effort from the salesperson to uncover any potential obstacles. Simply put, I don't ask questions to solicit the answer someone "thinks" I want to hear. Instead, my purpose in asking is to get the real answer.

Therefore, instead of fishing for good news by asking a hope-filled question like, "Are we still in good shape to get the deal?", I would be much more inclined to ask, *"Mr. Customer, do you think we're still in good shape to wrap this contract up by the end of the month, or is it possible that something might cause this deal to get pushed out?"*

Notice that I am actually inviting the customer to share bad news, if there is any. I don't actually want bad news, but I do want to know if the customer can foresee any obstacles that could prevent the opportunity from moving forward. Another way to neutralize this question would be to ask, *"Is there anything that might prevent you from moving forward on this decision?"* Can you see how these questions don't ask for good news? Instead, they seek the whole story.

Another variation of this technique would be to reverse roles in the conversation. Ask the customer, *"If you were the salesperson on this account, would you be doing anything differently?"* This question is neither hopeful or negative. It's completely neutral. In fact, this is one of the most insightful questions you can ask your customers, coworkers, boss, or employees. You may even want to ask your kids or your spouse, *"If our roles were reversed and you were me, what would you be doing differently?"* I guarantee that this question will generate some of the most accurate and valuable feedback you will ever receive. The only question now is, do you actually want to hear that feedback?

Work Backward from Implementation

Not long ago I had a conference call with a Sales VP who said, "Tom, I think we're going to postpone our plans for sales training for about six months." That struck me as funny. I understand that companies have expense budgets and timing issues that need to fall into place in order to bring people together for a corporate training event. And, I'm certainly not the only salesperson who has encountered a scenario where customers delay their decision until some point in the future.

But, let me tell you why this particular comment strikes me as being funny. When do you suppose is the best time to schedule a sales training course? Given the hustle and bustle of our fast paced business culture, it's never a "good time" for training. So, why would it ever make sense to bring in Question Based Selling? The only justifiable reason to schedule a QBS training course is to boost results. Therefore, if you don't expect a significant upside in terms of increased sales productivity, then you shouldn't bother to schedule one of our courses—*ever*! On the other hand, if you believe QBS would significantly increase your sales team's effectiveness and results, then why would you wait six more months to boost sales productivity?

Not surprisingly, few of our clients are motivated by my desire to deliver a QBS training event. Instead, most are motivated by their desire to accomplish specific business objectives—like filling the pipeline, creating differentiation in the marketplace, protecting profit margins, and closing business. Hence, the real question that should dictate when a client schedules training is: When would you like to start seeing results?

I encountered similar experiences when I sold technology solutions. Customers don't really care about when the salesperson receives the order. That's why I didn't spend much time hounding decision makers about when certain deals were going to close. Instead, I focused more on what needed to happen to ensure a successful implementation.

Working backward from specific implementation dates often made it easy to create a greater sense of urgency for moving forward. For example, if you were working on a telecommunication equipment sale, you could ask a customer, *"Mr. Prospect, if you can look past the initial purchase for a moment, when would you like to have this equipment installed and fully operational?"*

This is a valuable qualifying question. Like before, if the prospect hasn't even thought about their implementation timeframe, then they probably aren't close to making a purchase. Focusing on the timeframe for implementation rather than the status of the purchase order is also valuable because it allows the salesperson to follow up on the timing of a deal without making customers feel like they are being hounded for a transaction. Prospects are well aware that you want to consummate a sale, but they can only take so much pestering about when the actual order will be placed.

Suppose, for example, you inquired about the customer's implementation plans and the decision maker said, *"We would like to have the system up and running by January 15th."* If it's only September, January might seem like a long way off; in which case, people might drag their feet because there's no sense of urgency. Hence the value of working backwards from a specific date. With a couple quick calculations, you can increase the customer's sense of urgency by showing them that the window to make a decision is much shorter than they might think.

So, working backward from the customer's January 15th implementation date, I might ask, *"How much time should we allow for testing before the equipment goes into production?"* Few technology solutions are put into production on the very day they are received. A fully integrated solution needs to be staged, assembled, tested, installed, and then inspected, before being deemed ready for service.

"Let's allow six weeks total—two weeks to install hardware and thirty days to test our internal procedures," the prospect says.

I would continue working backward, by asking, *"Once you make a technical decision, how long do you think it will take to get the official signatures needed to cut a purchase order?"*

"Negotiating the contract could take a couple weeks, depending on the availability of the legal department, but once that's done, we can probably cut a PO fairly quickly," the prospect replies.

The next step is critical. Once you've identified the elements of the decision process, and you understand the lead-times involved, you simply work backward to construct a timeline by calculating how much time remains for the prospect to make a decision. I might summarize by saying: *"Mr. Prospect, if your system needs to be live on January 15th, and we need to allow six weeks for testing, two weeks for staging, and another two weeks for the holidays in December, we would need to have an order in hand the first week of November in order to meet your implementation schedule. Basically, that leaves thirty days to evaluate the product and make a decision."*

The net effect is a project that was slated to happen "sometime next year" suddenly requires a decision in the next thirty days. Can you see how this could foster a greater sense of urgency? As an added bonus, revising the customer's timeline places you in more of a consultative role. At that point, you are actually helping them to plan ahead and visualize the future, thus ensuring their project goes smoothly. That's way more valuable than just pestering customers to hurry up and make a decision.

Wrapping Up an Employment Interview

Now that we have talked about everything from piquing the prospect's curiosity, to establishing your credibility early in the sales process, needs development, positioning your value, and securing a commitment toward closure, let's take one more look at the metaphor of selling yourself in a job interview.

As I said in the beginning of the book, every formal employment interview is a sales situation, and every sales situation is a job interview. The comparison especially becomes apparent when you break the critical elements of the sales process down into the various component parts. Whether you are meeting a potential customer (or hiring manager) for the first time, or you are differentiating yourself from other qualified candidates, aligning your value to the customer's needs, or wrapping up the details of a transaction, the value of the products and services you offer is ultimately a reflection of the customer's perception of *you*. In that vein, you are always selling yourself.

Following your interview, you will either be offered a position or you won't. You have either made the sale, or you haven't. Granted, it may take a few days for the hiring manager to complete the current round of interviews or narrow the pool of candidates down to a short list. Your patience may be further tested by the bureaucracy we affectionately call Human Resources. But, at the end of the day, companies conduct employment interviews for a reason, and they are going to make a decision to go in some direction. Whether they choose you has a lot to do with your approach and how you have chosen to position yourself with the customer.

First impressions are still important. That's why we invested the time in earlier chapters to talk about bonding with potential customers on their problems (PAS), versus your solutions (SPA). If you have done your homework in advance, then you should have a pretty clear idea of what a hiring manager might want before you even darken their doorstep. This will enable you to pique the customer's interest and establish your own credibility.

Once you get the interview off to a strong start, it's easy then to look for a chance to ask, "Can I ask you a couple specifics about the opportunity?" On the heels of demonstrating that you are focused on helping the manager address their goals of a quick ramp up to full productivity quickly, blending with the existing culture, bringing new ideas and a fresh perspective to the team, etc., securing the customer's permission to ask "a couple specifics" will likely be music to an interviewer's ears.

In addition to being thoughtful enough to ask relevant and intelligent questions, hiring managers look for you to be interested in knowing more about the position. But, you can't just declare that you are interested in being hired. You must demonstrate your interest in the position. That's easy for the question-based salesperson, because there is no better way to show interest in a customer than to ask questions that demonstrate your knowledge and show that you have appropriately prepared in advance of the meeting. From the interviewer's perspective, there's a big difference between someone who knows what they want to ask, whose thoughtful questions seem to just roll off their tongue, and the nervously shallow candidate who is working hard to think of something relevant to say.

After reading this book, you will handle your next job interview, and all sales situations, much differently than before. You will let the other candidates competing for the position make the mistake of trying to claim their own credibility. You will know that the more they talk about themselves or their resume, the more they will end up commoditizing their value to the customer. You, on the other hand, will know how to secure the hiring manager's permission in advance to facilitate a free-flowing exchange of ideas and information

As your meeting winds down and the hiring manager asks if you have any more questions, you will have one. Using the *humbling disclaimer* technique we talked about earlier, you will say something like, *"I don't want to seem overly forthright or inappropriate in any way, but is it a fair question to ask your impression?"* Technically, the answer to this question is either "Yes (it is fair to ask), or, "No (that's not an appropriate question)." Before you even deliver the actual question, your understanding of *Conversational Dynamics* enables you to know that the hiring manager won't just answer with a simple yes or no. Instead, they will comfortably and openly share their impressions about you right then and there, and they will appreciate that you were forthright enough to ask. Of course, knowing where you stand is the first step to closing the sale.

Especially if you are interviewing for a sales position, the hiring manager will see that you are comfortable and willing to ask for the order. You will have also positioned yourself perfectly to be the one who is focused on helping the customer address their goals, objectives, issues, and concerns. I can tell you that you will be the only candidate who asked the hiring manager for permission at the beginning of the interview, and also, the only one who asks for their impression at the end. Note that it doesn't take courage or bravery to be successful if you put yourself in the position of having superior technique.

> "You will be the only candidate who asked the hiring manager for permission at the beginning of the interview, and for their impression at the end."

Who knows, you may get hired on the spot. You may also find out from the interviewer that there are a couple of gaps in your credentials relative to what the employer is looking for from the ideal candidate. Becoming aware of these gaps is actually a good thing. Remember, you can't address an issue you don't know about. Since there is no such thing as the perfect candidate anyway, the hiring manager's concern actually affords you a unique opportunity to reiterate your strengths and shore up any potential shortcomings while wrapping up the meeting. You can also echo key points in your subsequent correspondence.

As an extra bonus, asking the interviewer for their "impression" usually leads into some valuable expectation setting with regard to what happens next. Will the hiring decision be made in a matter of hours, days, or weeks? Will subsequent interviews be necessary to gain the support of other managers or key executives? Is there anything the interviewer would suggest you do in the meantime?

One of the biggest secrets to being successful in any kind of selling is having the knowledge and perspective to understand that potential customers are only going to share their thoughts, feelings, and concerns with some fraction of the sellers/candidates who are out there offering goods and services. Fortunately, for those sellers who are willing to demonstrate the level of commitment that you have shown by reading this entire book, the extent to which people will choose to deal with you has everything to do with your philosophy on *Selling Yourself in Today's Competitive Marketplace.*

Now it's up to you to put these proven strategies into practice, and go have some fun. Game on!

Paint Pictures with Your Words

Most people think in pictures, not words. Thus, if you want to be an excellent communicator, your words must enable customers to visualize the value of your products and services.

Painting pictures with words is an extremely valuable sales skill, but one that is generally left to the individual to figure out. As a bonus to all the other techniques we've discussed, let me show you how to convey more value with significantly less effort.

Words, words, words...so many words! Particularly in today's competitive marketplace, hungry sellers are always trying to out-describe each other, and the abundance of words (even fancy marketing words) has become so deafening that many of the claims vendors make about their products and services are instantly disregarded, if not totally ignored.

If you think about it, a vendor sales pitch is really just a bunch of empty words—that is, until the customer begins to visualize how the solutions being recommended could benefit their business, or benefit them personally.

The human mind doesn't actually visualize words, however. We visualize pictures. Perhaps you've heard the saying *a picture is worth a thousand words*. It's true. Try reading a short written paragraph describing something, and then look at a picture of the same item. When you see the visual image, your brain automatically begins to process specific shapes, color, shading, and depth. You'll also recognize and register special relationships and visual contrasts between the various objects that exist in the picture. Auto-emotional responses may also be triggered if you associate something in the picture with experiences you've had in the past. The neurons in your brain instantaneously go crazy when you see an actual picture rather than just hearing a bunch of words.

> "The neurons in your brain instantaneously 'go crazy' when you see an actual picture as opposed to just hearing a bunch of words."

Consider this. Have you ever noticed that you don't dream in words? You dream in pictures. When we sleep, there's no message ticker running across the bottom of the screen as if you were watching a cable news program. When you dream, it's more like watching a movie. Essentially, the subconscious mind enables us to visualize our thoughts.

During live QBS Training courses, I sometimes invite the audience to try an experiment. I say, "Close your eyes for a few moments and pretend you are walking across an expansive rolling meadow of green grass in the early springtime. In the background you see tall trees blowing in the wind, against a brilliant Carolina Blue sky dotted with large billowy clouds. In the foreground, you see a single flower standing tall against the surrounding green grass. As you approach, the flower turns out to be a long-stemmed daisy, its circular fan of brilliant white petals surrounding a yellowish-orange center."

Then, I say, "Now open your eyes. Did you actually see the word D-A-I-S-Y, or did you visualize a picture of a daisy?" I already know the answer—people tend to think in pictures, not just words.

The ability to eloquently verbalize ideas and concepts is rapidly becoming a lost art in our modern society. Given the accelerating pace of life, coupled with our ever-narrowing attention spans, much of the information that is now communicated is netted out into a list of succinct bullet points. As a result, the art of story telling is quickly being replaced by the practice of condensing one's thoughts down into a few cryptic words that can be texted or emailed.

If you want prospective buyers to recognize the full value of your product or service, then your company's story and the messages you want to convey must be articulated in a way that creates visual images in the minds of your target audience. You do this by painting pictures with words. Essentially, this is the skill of story telling.

Better Relate to Your Audience

The underlying themes that drive any sales process are pretty basic. Sellers ultimately want to convey the value of their offerings to potential buyers, and decision makers want to understand their alternatives in order to choose the best solution.

Perhaps the most important lesson about relating to your audience has been driven home several times already in the book. Let me ask again: What is more important to the typical customer when you first engage—their problems (P), issues, and concerns, or your solutions (S)? The core of our positioning philosophy in Question Based Selling is the foundational thought that you bond with potential buyers on what's most important to them (P), rather than what's important to you (S).

We also talked about leveraging specific conversational techniques like mini-invitations, diagnostic questions, and escalating the strategic focus of your questions to increase the value of your needs development conversations.

One of the best ways to actually communicate with people as you execute the various steps in the sales process is to leverage stories, anecdotes, metaphors, analogies, and parables to explain or enhance key points you want to make. Just open to any chapter in each of the books I've published (including this one), and you will notice that I rely on some form of explanation device to paint for the reader a more in-depth picture of the concepts I am trying to convey.

The purpose of using stories is to better relate to your audience, plain and simple. Ultimately in sales, you're trying to translate the capabilities and potential benefits of your recommended solution into real value for the customer. Given that most people who evaluate your product or service are comparative thinkers, they will naturally try to put your value proposition in context, mostly likely by relating it to something they already familiar with or understand.

For example, when I explained earlier that using *diagnostic questions* to kick off your needs development conversations will open the floodgates of communication, there are no gates that really open. Opening the floodgates is just a figure of speech.

However, the expression is valuable because of the image it conveys to the reader. It communicates that the technique of using diagnostic questions will act as a catalyst to initiate an impressive flow of information.

Speaking of floods, I am yet to train a sales organization that actually sells water pumps. Nonetheless, I take virtually every student through a hypothetical planning exercise to discuss the do's and don'ts of how best to position yourself if you were selling a water pump. I use this analogy to intentionally separate sellers from whatever details and nuances may have affected their last deal. This allows us to focus exclusively on strategy and sales technique. Once you understand how to extrapolate the customer's issues into more specific implications, and you have a handle on the logic of PAS positioning versus the traditional SPA approach, the lessons learned using the water pump metaphor can be adapted to virtually any sales situation.

From my perspective, a better understanding of the underlying concepts leads to quicker action, whether we're talking about a student of mine putting QBS techniques into practice, or a potential customer of yours deciding to move forward with a purchase.

For example, in the first chapter of my first book, I draw a parallel between dating and selling, where I refer to dating as *the ultimate sale* because it represents *the ultimate risk*. Has my advice actually helped unmarried people have more success in their respective dating careers? I bet it has. More importantly, the risk reduction strategies built into Question Based Selling have helped thousands of salespeople to fill the pipeline with more prospective customers, navigate more effective sales conversations, and significantly improve their chances of success in the sales process.

Even the metaphor I used to characterize *your next job interview* has a much broader application in this book, which extends way beyond just an employment interview.

Take your pick—whether we're talking about *Gold Medals* and *German Shepherds*, my first home buying experience, or *The Wizard of Oz*, you can bring your stories to life by creatively weaving relevant anecdotes, metaphors, analogies, and parables into the context of the messages you're trying to convey. I always say that relating to your audience is a function of distilling concepts and philosophies down to the customer conversation level. If the person who is on the receiving end of your words thinks, "I've had something like that happen to me before," the point you are trying to make will forever be cemented in their mind.

Specificity Brings Your Messages to Life

Hopefully, you do have a good story to tell about your products, services, and the company that supports them. Your ability to actually tell the story in a compelling manner, however, will largely determine the degree to which you are able to impact potential buyers.

Some people are natural story-tellers. When they speak, everybody listens. These people are said to have a certain charm, personality, or charisma. What they really possess is the secret to being a good story-teller. Nobody talks about it, but there's definitely something that makes their messages more compelling than others. The secret to effective story telling is *specificity*.

One of the quickest and easiest adjustments a salesperson can make is to replace standard clichés, industry buzzwords, and higher level promotional sound bites with more specific details. I'm not suggesting that you should be more technical when describing your product, just more colorful and detailed in how you convey your descriptions and key points.

I can't give you an exact formula for how much color to add in your conversations, but I can give you an example. Watch what happens when the same thing is said in two different ways below. Can you spot the difference?

Option A: *"I went to the store and rented a movie."*

Option B: *"After I devoured a nine ounce fillet that my wife Laura cooked for me on the patio grill last night, my two daughters and I hopped into the van and cruised down to the local supermarket (a mile from my house) to rent a Disney movie to watch on our big screen TV."*

Which version of the truth paints a more vivid picture of what happened last night? Obviously the answer is Option B, because it provides a more detailed depiction. In a single sentence, we now know when the events occurred, what I ate for dinner, who went with me to the grocery store, how far the supermarket is from my house, what kind of car I drove, and our purpose in making the trip. We even know what kind of movie was rented, and where it was watched.

While it's true that a picture does paint a thousand words, a thousand words can also paint a pretty clear picture. The goal here is not to be verbose, just more compelling. Let me give you an example of how this notion of increased specificity can be applied to the sales process.

Seller: *"Speaking of customer references, Emory University Hospital initially deployed an earlier version of our inventory system in March 2004, back when John Thompson had just become Director of Materials Management. They recently upgraded again in November 2008, and they are getting ready to install three other financial modules. In fact, I had lunch with the COO from Emory two weeks ago at the Atlanta Chamber of Commerce meeting, where the speaker ironically talked about delivering government funded healthcare programs versus the private sector."*

The seller in this example could have just said something cursory, like, "Emory is one of our best customers." So, why am I suggesting you even bother to say all those extra words, when you can say essentially the same thing much more concisely?

One of our jobs as salespeople is to educate potential buyers on the value of our solutions. Consequently, there is some responsibility on our part to communicate the relevant facts about the products and services we offer. Another important responsibility of the salesperson is to make customers feel comfortable that they are making a good decision. While partial or incomplete information from a seller tends to make customers feel less comfortable, the opposite is also true. Bottom line, the clearer the customer's vision, the more comfortable they will feel with regard to moving forward.

What's the alternative to being purposeful and specific? Being generic? Particularly when you want to talk with customers about issues they face or the implications of those issues, very few customers have generic problems and even less are looking for high-level generic solutions.

The Art of Question Based Selling

I definitely believe there is some science behind having a repeatable model that maximizes your sales effectiveness. That's partly what has motivated me to write five books on the subject. But, I would point out that there is also an art to being a successful communicator.

The science includes understanding the underlying logic that enables sellers to manage the *Scope, Focus,* and *Disposition* of their questions, such that they ask the right question at the right time. The science also includes a toolkit of communication techniques like *Global Questions, Conversational Dynamics, Conversational Layering, The Herd Theory, Diagnostic Questions, Building a Mutual Agenda,* and *closing on appropriate next steps* in the sales process.

The artistic portion of sales communication is in choosing the actual words that either best deliver the questions you want to ask, or best conveys your value proposition. Like a painter standing in front of a canvas, holding a palette with the full spectrum of colors from which to choose, you must color and blend your words to create the picture you desire. A salesperson's ability to articulate their message by creating visual images with words will likely determine the customer's perception of your value, their comfort level, and where you stand relative to competitors who are also vying for marketshare.

The best advice I can give you about articulating a valuable message is to think less about what you are trying to say, and more about what the customer wants (or needs) to hear from you in order to move forward with a favorable decision. If the roles were reversed and you were the customer, what is it that you would need to hear from a vendor in your industry to feel comfortable that you are choosing the right solution? Would you form the impression that you were dealing with a knowledgeable, thoughtful, credible resource, or just another salesperson pushing their wares? There is definitely an art to communicating in a way that best aligns with the customer's perspective.

Let everyone else talk in terms of sound bites and high level generalities. But, you make a personal commitment to yourself and to your customers that if you take the time to say it, you will also take the time to explain it. Helping customers clearly see the value of your solutions by describing them in more creative ways is a tremendously valuable selling skill, one that will make the difference time and time again.

For Sales Managers Only

What's the definition of insanity? Maybe it's insane to write five 'how to' books for a target audience that isn't always open to hearing constructive feedback. Do you know any salespeople with big egos? Ah, but how quickly things can change, especially now that so many sellers have been humbled by recent market conditions, coupled with the realization that your success moving forward will likely require some modifications to your current approach.

Never before have salespeople or sales organizations been so hungry for change or for a fresh set of ideas that will help their customers, colleagues, and company, in addition to helping themselves. In fact, the status quo might be a salesperson's worst enemy at this point, as current clients are reevaluating their existing vendor agreements and new opportunities will be predictably more difficult to penetrate. It's just not logical to believe that the whole business climate is changing, but your sales approach can remain the same and still get results.

But sales are still going to happen, and you have to figure that someone is going to earn the customer's confidence and ultimately win the business. That person might as well be you. Herein lies my point—your success in the future will have more to do with your own personal effectiveness than ever before, and the notion of change can no longer be thought of as a motivational buzzword.

It's easy to *talk about* adapting to a new economy. The challenge for sales organizations is, there's never a "good time" for training. I hear it from salespeople and managers who have monthly, quarterly, and annual sales objectives they are desperately trying to meet. I am neither surprised nor offended that sitting in a sales training class isn't near the top of anyone's fun to do list. If I had a nickel for every time I felt this way when I was as a salesperson, I wouldn't have to write any more books. People are busy, and there probably won't ever be a convenient time to put your proverbial tools down long enough to sharpen your saw.

Even though I'm a sales trainer by trade, I would quickly tell you that this is *not* the time to revert back to traditional approaches. Instead, this *New Era of Salesmanship* may be the perfect opportunity for sellers to leverage logic, innovation, and update their skills, rather than simply gravitating back to old habits that will commoditize your value and make you sound just like everyone else.

My beef with the corporate establishment comes when salespeople are given lofty sales quotas, but then left to their own devices to figure out how to achieve such monumental goals. With the exception of the previous experiences sellers bring to the table, not much detail about how to be effective in this new environment is being provided. Most salespeople don't need motivation and encouragement. They need coaching and direction, and they need it *now*. One of the secrets in my first sales book simply states: *In order to have above average sales results, one must first be open to thinking about above average concepts.*

Sellers must do everything in their power to make themselves invaluable to their customers, colleagues, and their company. This will require a conscious effort on the individual's part to hunker down and honestly evaluate your current sales process, strategic mindset, and interpersonal skills. Can you change or adapt without having to wait for the rest of your sales team to get on board? Of course, you can. The question is, are you ready and willing to do what is necessary to take your game to the next level?

We have reached a defining moment where companies will be handsomely rewarded by part-nering with their sales teams to leverage the current appetite for change to your advantage. Identifying *what* to do and *how* to do it more effectively, should dominate your strategic focus moving forward. Building a cohe-sive sales strategy that the entire team can rally around, and then seeing perceptible results, is going to be the key to success. The good news is, most salespeople will respond very favorably if you can just light a fire under their competitive spirit.

> "Sellers must do everything in their power to make them-selves invaluable to customers, colleagues, and their company."

At the end of the day, a hungry salesperson combined with a proven methodology for differentiating your strategic sales efforts, creates the competitive advantage demanded by today's market.

Let me know how we can help.

About the Author

Thomas A. Freese, Founder and President of QBS Research, Inc., originally developed Question Based Selling as a methodology to differentiate salespeople and sales organizations from the rest of the "noise" in the marketplace. Now, as a dynamic speaker, trainer, and author of five books, Tom has become one of the foremost authorities on sales effectiveness training, buyer motivation, and business strategy.

Having spent the bulk of his career in the trenches of sales and management, Tom Freese recognized several fundamental problems with traditional sales approaches, starting with the fact that customers don't want to be pushed, probed, or pressured by a salesperson. People love to make wise purchase decisions, but no one wants to be "sold."

Especially in the current business climate, how you choose to position your company and products is important, but what's even more important is your ability to effectively position yourself. *Selling Yourself in Today's Competitive Marketplace*, therefore, has evolved as a natural next step in Tom's life's work to reestablish the sales professional as a valuable resource who can help customers accomplish their goals and objectives.

When he is not on the road delivering QBS methodology training or speaking at a conference, Tom and his wife Laura live in Atlanta with their two daughters, Sarah and Mary Claire.

Register for QBS OnLine™

You can now leverage the power of the Internet to license QBS OnLine, a highly interactive web-based training program that brings the Question Based Selling™ methodology right to your fingertips.

Multi-media learning:

In addition to clearly presented onscreen content, QBS OnLine features numerous brief video and audio clips, plus animated charts and diagrams. As well, its 'Notepad' feature allows you to jot down your own thoughts and ideas at any time and review them later.

Applicable to all major industries:

Rather than using abstract explanations, QBS OnLine presents typical business issues and contains sample questions and benefit statements for such industry categories as financial services, real estate, healthcare, packaged goods, pharmaceutical, high-tech, manufacturing and professional services.

Upgrade your current sales tools:

At various points during QBS OnLine, you're asked to describe some of your current sales practices. As you progress, you revisit - and improve - these initial entries, thus building your own arsenal of highly effective and fully customized sales tools.

Plenty of realistic examples:

Instead of just telling you how to accomplish a specific skill, QBS OnLine is filled with realistic scenarios, sample questions and model conversations to assist your learning.

Frequent quizzes:

Within each module, you'll find several mini-quizzes or matching exercises that reinforce key points. Each module also concludes with about a dozen multiple-choice questions that test your learning. In every case, the correct answers are clearly explained, further supporting your understanding and growth.

Other helpful navigation aids:

The program's "Bookmarking" feature enables you to pause at any point and return to that exact spot next time you open the program. A comprehensive 'Glossary' helps you understand all the key terms and concepts, while the powerful 'Search' function helps you find all the references to each selling principle.

QBS Audio Programs

Repetition is a critical success factor in any implementation. That's why QBS is also available on CDs. If you don't have a lot of time to read books, or if you spend a fair amount of time in the car on the way to visit customers or to and from work, then this audio program is definitely for you!

Visit: www.QBSresearch.com

The Question Based Parent
by Thomas A. Freese

What qualifies someone to write a parenting book? While that is certainly a reasonable question, this book isn't actually about parenting. There are lots of traditional parenting books already. *The Question Based Parent* is a communications book.

Before my wife and I had two daughters, I didn't have any idea what parenting might be like. Truthfully, nothing can adequately prepare you for the awesome responsibility of raising a child in today's world. Of course, every responsible parent wants to end up with well-behaved, respectful, confident and considerate children. To achieve this goal, however, there is some your responsibility on your part to be an effective communicator.

The Question Based Parent was written to put some methodology to the madness in our daily quest to raise impressive kids. Even if your children are the beneficiaries of  good genes, it must be noted that children are incapable of parenting themselves. Fortunately, there is no need to reinvent the wheel as many of the lessons that have been learned from the school of hard knocks can be immediately applied to make us better communicators and better parents.

The secret to successful communication is simple. It's *you*.

Other Books by Author

It all started with *Secrets of Question Based Selling*, which continues to be the core of the QBS methodology. Tom Freese recognized early on that it's easy to ask lots of questions. But, if someone chooses not to share with you, it doesn't really matter what questions you ask. Thus, the real skill in selling is causing people to "want to" engage with a salesperson they don't yet know and trust.

QBS has since evolved into a body of work that includes the two bestselling books: *It Only Takes 1% to Have a Competitive Edge in Sales* and *The New Era of Salesmanship,* and now... *Selling Yourself in Today's Competitive Marketplace.*

Visit: www.QBSresearch.com

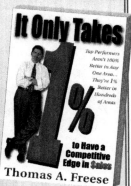

Contact Information

To schedule a customized QBS Methodology Training for your sales team, or if you would like more information about QBS books, Audio CDs, Coaching, or QBS Licensing, please contact us directly at:

QBS Research, Inc.
5600 Spalding Drive, 922933
Atlanta, GA   30092
Ofc: (770) 840-7640
Fax: (770) 840-7642
Email: admin@QBSresearch.com
Website: www.QBSresearch.com